GRAD TO GREAT

Dalidaze

Press

The authors wish to note that the names and personal details of some people interviewed for this book have been changed to protect their privacy. Internet addresses given in this book were accurate at the time of printing.

Published by Dalidaze Press
1400 W. Devon Ave, Suite 407
Chicago, IL 60660

Printed in Minneapolis, MN

Design by Brian Fugate of www.deliciousmission.com

Publisher's Cataloging-in-Publication

Brown, Anne, 1975-

    Grad to great / Anne Brown & Beth Zefo. -- Chicago, IL :
    Dalidaze Press, c2007.

        p. ; cm.

        ISBN: 978-0-9798018-0-8
        Includes bibliographical references.

        1. Job hunting. 2. Vocational guidance. 3. Career development.

    4. Young adults--Vocational guidance. I. Zefo, Beth. II. Title.

HF5381 .B76 2007

650.14/0842--dc22   0711

To my folks, for encouraging me to keep writing.
To my husband, Aaron, for making everything wonderful
and so worthwhile.
–Anne

To my parents, for always believing in me.
To my husband, Derek, for challenging me to be better,
and for your unconditional love and support.
–Beth

*The young do not know enough to be prudent,
and therefore they attempt the impossible—
and achieve it, generation after generation.*

Pearl S. Buck

CONTENTS

ACKNOWLEDGMENTS

Many people provided valuable input and encouragement during the process of writing this book, including Carrie Greenway, Jamie Spindler, Anne Copeland, Leah Shaheen, Jenny Hanawalt, Amy Dragoo, Michael Daly, Karyn McCoy, Kim King, Joe Brockseker, Melissa Blair, Bo Sandine, Amanda Amadei, Bill Brown and Carmen Brown. We are especially grateful to Derek Zefo, Janelle Kearsley, Jan D'Arcy, Greg Pryor, Dr. Joseph Johnston, Amanda Nell, Chris Ksoll, Kelley Amadei, Cam Marston and Rob Engelman. We are indebted to our talented graphic designer Brian Fugate. This book would not have been possible without our wonderful editors Jennifer Berk, Donna Brockseker and Mick Bechtel. Finally we would like to give a very special thanks to Aaron Brown for assisting us with the layout for the book.

INTRODUCTION

There are countless definitions of the term "success," but ultimately only one that matters—yours. How you define success in your own life will create the way you live your life.

If money is important to you, then you will pursue a job that includes a high-paying salary; success will be defined by how much wealth you accumulate. If exploring new places is important to you, then you will be attracted to opportunities that allow you to travel; success will be defined by how many countries you visit. If owning your own company is important to you, then you will look for ways to learn more about potential markets; success will be defined by the profitability of your business. No matter what your priority is right now, the key to achieving it is knowing you have what it takes to succeed. Believe in yourself and enlist others in your quest for success.

Once you know what you want, you also have to know how to ask for it, and you must be able to recruit others to help you. The primary aim of this book is to help you achieve success—as you define it—by teaching you how to articulate and communicate to others what exactly it is you want.

In *Grad to Great* we will explain how to motivate potential employers to hire you. We will share tips and secrets for communicating with colleagues and supervisors so they become interested in helping you achieve success. Most importantly, we'll show you how to apply these new communications skills in your everyday life to enable you to pursue your dreams and reach your goals.

We wrote this book to help you find and realize the career you want. It doesn't matter if you don't have much experience right now. It's not the number of years of experience you have at a job that makes you qualified for a position, it's how you use the knowledge you have. You are the only person who has had the experience of living your life. You have seen, done, and experienced things in a different way than anyone on earth. How you define and project that uniqueness will determine whether you are offered employment opportunities as well as other opportunities throughout your life. If you're willing to work hard and be your authentic self, you will get a job, you will excel at that job, and you will be successful.

Remember that all challenges are opportunities. Planning your career is one of the biggest challenges you'll ever have. If you can learn to put yourself across to others sincerely and professionally, there is nothing to stop you from achieving your life goals. If you are willing to throw your fears aside and approach each new challenge straight on, you can go from Grad to Great!

A Note About Grammar

In an attempt to be politically correct regarding gender, we have opted to use plural pronouns such as "them," "they," or "their" in several places where singular pronouns would have been grammatically correct. In passages where the use of plural pronouns would have diluted the point of our message, we did revert to the use of singular pronouns.

I

DO WHAT YOU LOVE, LOVE WHAT YOU DO

> *"Success is not the key to happiness.*
> *Happiness is the key to success.*
> *If you love what you are doing,*
> *you will be successful."*

Dr. Albert Schweitzer

The most overwhelming question you will ever ask yourself is, "What do I want to do with my life?" but there is a better and much simpler question to ask. This chapter explains what that question is and why answering it truthfully can help you find your ideal job. You'll also learn how to set goals so you can land the job you want and live the life you desire.

It's your final year of college. You wake up one morning and it hits you. This is it—the last year of college before you enter the real world. Suddenly, everything around you looks different. You begin to notice the senior class is divided into two distinct camps. In one camp everyone knows exactly what they want to do when they graduate. Some have known it their whole lives and others even have job offers. Everybody is calm and serene. In the other camp, nobody knows what they want to do after graduation. Far from having job offers, some may have just settled on a major. In this camp, there's a real sense of panic.

Take us for example: sisters Beth and Anne. At 17, Beth knew she wanted to be an engineer. As a kid she was always taking things apart and putting them back together—very often successfully. Beth applied to two universities with excellent engineering colleges. She chose one, completed her program, and had two paid internships under her belt by the time she received her diploma. She received a job offer from General Motors during her senior year and negotiated a late start date so she could travel around the world for four months before she began. Ten years later, she's still with General Motors.

On the other hand, Anne switched majors three times. Junior year she finally settled on English, but still didn't have a clear idea of what she wanted to do or what she would even be qualified to do after college. With her guidance counselor on sabbatical her senior year, she turned to a book that claimed you could find your perfect career by studying your fingerprints. Several ink pads later, she was no closer to a career choice, but she did ace her elective in criminology. Eleven years later she's self-employed and enjoying success in the communications industry.

If you know what you're interested in, your path is clearer because you have a focus. You can go online and research the companies you're interested in. You can ask the staff at the career center for their insight as to which companies hire students most like you: your GPA, interests, geographical preference, whatever. You can talk to family and friends who know people at companies you're interested in and ask for informational interviews. You can go directly to the company and request to visit the facilities. You have numerous options available to you. (See Chapter 2 for more job search tips.) But if you're one of the much larger group of people who don't know what you want to do, or even what you're interested in, your path can be more difficult to navigate. It is to this group that we dedicate the rest of this chapter.

What if I Don't Know What I'm Interested In

To find out what interests you—what you're passionate about—experience as many different things as you can. There is no other way to know what you like and what you don't. If you can't think of anything that sounds exciting to you, get out there and have more experiences. Unless it's your dream job, fight the urge to take the first entry-level job that comes along because chances are you'll be miserable within six months.

If you are in a serious rut and nothing seems to stimulate you, do something you're terrified of. Get out of your comfort zone because there really is nothing more empowering than conquering fear. Embrace the unknown. Think of it as another learning opportunity.

There are many things you can do to get the ball rolling: talk to friends; take a class; join a book club; go to a wine tasting; volunteer at a shelter; do a 10K run. Do anything to interact with other people. Talk with them and find out what they like to do and what experiences they've had that you would like to try.

Additionally, you can narrow down your interests by making a list of what you don't want to do. Think back to jobs, assignments, or even school projects and subjects that you disliked. Put those on the list of things you definitely don't want to do. Think of it as your "To-Don't" list.

You can also think about people you admire. Why do you admire them? What kinds of things are they interested in? Do any of those interests appeal to you?

What if I Know What I'm Interested In?

Perhaps you know what you're interested in, but not how it translates into a job. You love writing, but don't think you can get a job at a magazine. You want to be a buyer for a department store, but have no idea how to get your foot in the door. You want to be a professor but don't have the best grades so graduate school seems out of your reach. Don't let any of this stop you from pursuing your dream.

Go talk to people. Talk to as many you can find who will listen. Go to the career center. Tell your counselors, professors, family and friends that you know what you want to do and enlist their help in finding a job. Don't worry about your major, and don't worry if you aren't a 4.0 student. Employers are looking for people who know what they want to do and they're surprisingly hard to find. If you're someone who knows what you want to do, don't be shy about speaking up. If people understand what it is you want to accomplish, they may offer to help you, or even hire you. The key in approaching people is to be assertive, but not aggressive or cocky.

What If I Have Too Many Interests?

After identifying your interests, you are now ready to start searching for a job. What if you're having a hard time figuring out what to do because you have too many interests? Realize that having several interests is never bad. It indicates that you are naturally curious and being curious means you are more likely to explore multiple fields and industries thereby mitigating the risk of choosing a job you will not enjoy. Since several opportunities will appeal to you, however, your main challenge will be to find a position that won't bore you after a few months, because you will always be on the lookout for new challenges.

Talk to people in the various fields and industries you're considering. Talk to professors that teach those subjects.

"When choosing a career, be aware that you're not going to love everyday at your job. The key is to choose a career that is gratifying overall and will allow you to enjoy your personal life. For me, this includes the ability to take time off, ability to make enough income to support my spending habits, and in the end a career that doesn't compromise my ethics. Also, I wish I'd known when I was starting out that every job, regardless if it is corporate, nonprofit, large or small, has internal politics."

Senior Account Executive in Paper Industry
Age: 39
University of Memphis

Table 1.1

What Types Of Students Are Job Recruiters Looking For?	
Well-rounded	3.5 GPA, leadership experience, successfully completed an internship
Strong Communicators	Written and verbal
Team Oriented	Knows how to be a contributor
Bilingual	Increasingly companies are looking for students who speak two languages
Honest	Integrity and honesty are often in the top 3–4 traits most valued by recruiters
Self-aware	Recruiters want students who know what is considered "professional" on the job

Source: Interview with Professor of Counseling Psychology
and Director of the Career Center at
University of Missouri-Columbia,
Dr. Joseph Johnston

They can be particularly helpful if you love the subject you majored in, but aren't sure how it translates into a job. Sometimes professors also do consulting work on the side. Politely ask them what companies they do consulting work for. These companies may be a good fit for you in particular—you are a student of their consultant. Even if they aren't willing, or able, to tell you the names of the particular companies they work with, they'll probably be happy to share what types of companies they work with.

You can also make a list of all your interests and skills. Compare your list to job descriptions on Internet job sites. Don't focus on job titles: concentrate on the actual job descriptions. Which jobs match your interests and skills the closest? Apply for those positions.

If you receive positive responses from several companies, make time to interview with all of them. Not only is this good experience, but also there's no sense limiting your options before you've explored them. You may make contacts beneficial to you in the future.

What Do I Want To Do Right Now?

You leave college with two things: a diploma, and a huge pile of debt. Some people will tell you this is a good reason to forget about pursuing your interests and follow the money instead. Hogwash! If you are going to spend the next several years paying off school loans, you have more reason than anyone to find something you love right from the start.

Instead of putting senseless pressure on yourself to figure out what you want to do for the rest of your life, just ask yourself, "What do I want to do right now?" That's the real question you need to answer. What sounds particularly interesting to you at this moment?

We have a friend, Jennifer, who graduated from the Massachusetts Institute of Technology in 2002. After moving to Chicago she decided to spend six months considering which career to pursue without worrying too much about finding a job. Six months later Jennifer still had no idea what she wanted to do. Convinced that she just needed to start doing something, she began to look for a job—any job. She only had one criterion: it had to involve computers.

After answering an ad on Craig's List, Jennifer was offered a temp position at an interactive media company. After a month the company offered her an internship, which paid better than the temp position and provided more interesting work. A few months later—after proving herself—Jennifer was hired full-time and promoted to Programmer.

She went on to become the company's first Information Architect. This is an exciting new field that involves consulting with clients to determine how best to organize their web sites. Jennifer hadn't even heard of information architecture when she graduated. If she had not decided to go ahead and try something that seemed interesting, she wouldn't be where she is today.

When Jennifer started her job search all she knew was that she liked computers, but she had no idea what kind of career she wanted. She answered an Internet ad for a temp position simply because it sounded interesting to her. She followed her intuition; her gut feeling. Now she has found a career she loves—all because she followed her heart and just put herself out there. She asked, "What do I want to do right now?" You can do this same thing.

Go With Your Gut Feeling—It's Seldom Wrong

Once you identify your interests, your next step is to pursue a job that most closely aligns with them. Don't allow anyone else's opinion or criticism to sway you. You can listen to what they have to say, but you must follow your own path if you want to experience happiness and job satisfaction. In September of 2006, Oprah Winfrey was the keynote speaker at the twentieth anniversary celebration luncheon for the Women's Business Development Center located in Chicago. During her speech she told an inspiring story about getting hired as a reporter at a TV news station early in her career.

The management at the station wanted her to change her name to something they said was "more familiar" like Sally or Susan. Oprah decided she would not change her name. Instead, the TV station would have to decide how to make her name work. They ran several promos before Oprah went on the air. The ads depicted local reporters asking people around town, "Do you know what an Oprah is?" Well, today the world definitely knows and they know her as Oprah—not as Sally Sue—because she followed her gut instinct. In her speech she said there were three key things that helped her get to where she is today:

1. Using intuition and following gut instinct.

2. Doing everything with intention.

3. Following her passions.

Above all else, you should trust yourself. After that, every action you take should be with intention—with the purpose of reaching your goals. Finally, do what you are passionate about, not what someone else tells you to care about. Do these three things and you will live an authentic life.

Set Goals

James Cash Penney, founder of the J.C. Penney department store, once said, "Give me a stock clerk with a goal and I'll give you a man who will make history. Give me a man with no goals and I'll give you a stock clerk."

"I am now on my third career path. I have followed the money and have followed the 'freedom' of being an entrepreneur and I honestly cannot tell you which one is better. They each have *very* strong advantages. I am glad I followed the money because it gave me the opportunity to go out on a limb with our business. I think you truly have to adapt to what 'feels' right at the time. Do not over analyze or focus on the future because you can always change if it starts to not 'feel right' down the road. In other words, do not be afraid of change or failure and do not become a prisoner to anything by becoming so attached that you lose yourself (this relates to both work and play)."

Real Estate Professional
Age: 30
University of Tennessee

Having goals is important if you want to be successful. Goals indicate that you have the ambition to achieve something. They signify that you want something more for your life and that you have something to strive for. Goals provide you with direction, purpose, focus, and hope. Having goals also gives you more control over achieving the level of success you want in your life.

Goal setting is a process that makes achieving your long-term vision possible and much less daunting. You stay motivated and achieve success faster by breaking down your big goals into smaller, more manageable short-term goals.

It's important to identify and make lists of both your long and short-term goals. Long-term goals generally take several years to accomplish. There is not much you can do to speed up the timeline that will be required to achieve these types of goals. Some long-term goal examples:

★ Becoming a doctor

★ Repairing bad credit

★ Saving money for down payment on a house

★ Having a successful career

On the other hand, short-term goals can usually be achieved within one year or less. These goals can often be reached sooner if you prioritize your time wisely and limit distractions. For example, let's say you want to learn how to snowboard or play the guitar. To become skilled at either of these activities, you'll need to devote your free time to practicing instead of doing other things. Your success will be determined by how much time you invest.

Table 1.2

Goals	Unspecific	Specific
Long-term	I will get a more advanced degree than I have now.	By December 31, 2012 I will have received my PhD in Psychology from Northwestern University.
Short-term	I'll get a job.	Within the next three months I'll get a job in accounting with one of the top four firms.

Examples of short-term goals might include:

★ Learning how to play golf

★ Getting a certificate in time management

★ Completing a pottery class

★ Getting a job

As you are writing down your goals, be sure to be specific. Write down precisely what you intend to accomplish and when you plan to achieve it. Use the examples in Table 1.2 to help you brainstorm.

1. Identify your long and short-term goals

2. Write them down

3. Be specific in your wording

4. Keep your goals where you can view them frequently

5. Celebrate each success, no matter how small

Do everything with the intention of reaching your goals. Think about the choices you make every day. Continue with actions that propel you towards your goals and cease making choices that push them further away. Stay focused until you achieve the result that makes you happy and make sure to celebrate each time you reach one of your goals.

When you find something you really want to do, something you truly are passionate about, go for it. Your efforts now will pay big dividends later in ways you cannot yet imagine. That is what makes the journey so exciting and worthwhile.

"You don't have to take the first job opportunity that comes along simply because you are just starting out. Unless an opportunity excites you, or has the potential to move you closer to your goals, don't take it. It will only trap you and dampen your motivation."

Personal Fitness Trainer &
Prenatal Exercise Specialist
Age: 30
University of Illinois at Urbana-Champaign

Chapter Summary

★ Most people don't know exactly what they want to do right out of college. Don't worry if you're still finding your path.

★ Figure out what you're passionate about. Try new things and gain as much experience in life as you can; this is the only way to discover your interests.

★ Let your interests guide your job search. Ask yourself not "What do I want to do for the rest of my life?" but "What do I want to do right now?"

★ Always go with your gut instinct. Do not let others dissuade you from following your own path. Stay true to yourself.

★ Set specific goals and you'll be more likely to achieve them.

★ Seek to understand what motivates you. Then find a job that will reward you in kind.

★ If you are good at your job, and passionate about it, you will be successful.

2

KNOW YOURSELF

"Be aware of yourself and know yourself.
No matter how much you have learned
and how much you know,
if you don't know yourself you don't know anything."

The Japanese Art of War
Thomas Cleary

Before going to job interviews there are several important questions you need to ask yourself. In this chapter you'll have the opportunity to answer seven questions that make up the Grad to Great™ Personal Inventory. You'll also discover why it's important to know yourself—well—before interviewing.

Alyssa had just landed the job interview of her dreams with one of the largest consulting firms in the country. After seeing an online notice that the company was coming to campus to interview students from the business school, Alyssa, a liberal arts student, sent the human resources department her resumé and called to ask if she could interview even though she wasn't a business major. She was a dual major in history and sociology. The HR staff member that Alyssa spoke with said, "Of course." He was delighted she had taken the initiative to call and told her she could interview with Ellen, the on-campus recruiter, in three days.

For the following three days Alyssa told all her friends and family how excited she was about the interview. She typed up her resumé and printed it on nice paper. She had her interviewing suit dry-cleaned and hung it neatly in her closet. She got a haircut and bought some conservative shoes to match her suit. She researched the company on-line and memorized almost every word on their web site. She even planned out her route to the interview site so she'd be certain to arrive ten minutes early. She was ready for her interview.

Ellen was new at the consulting firm. This would be only her second trip to conduct on-campus interviews. Her job performance over the next year would be judged by how well she selected candidates that fit in well at the firm. Managers were counting on Ellen to find not only the best talent, but also to choose candidates that are likely to re-main at the firm for several years, which is generally con-sidered the amount of time it takes to have a real impact at this company. It is a big responsibility, and one that Ellen took seriously.

The time to start the interview arrived. As they shook hands and introduced themselves, Ellen noticed that Alyssa was wearing a nice suit and that she had taken care to print her resumé on nice paper. Ellen was impressed. She motioned for Alyssa to have a seat and asked her first question.

"If you had your choice, which division of our company would most interest you and why?"

Alyssa's mind was now racing. She mentally scrolled through all the pages of the company's web site and found the page she needed.

"Well, you have unmatched expertise in 14 different industries and offices in just about every major city in the US and around the world. Um, honestly, I'd be happy anywhere."

Ellen's heart sank. She was expecting a much better answer. "Alyssa, there are major differences between those industries; do you have one or two that would interest you more than others?"

Alyssa started to panic. She had been hoping Ellen could tell her what her dual major in history and sociology qualified her to do at the firm. She didn't have a clue what team she would most likely fit in with and she wasn't expecting to have to know.

Ellen was ready to end the interview. She knew she couldn't bring Alyssa to the firm for a second interview—at least not until Alyssa had a clear idea of what she could contribute to a specific division.

How can Alyssa redeem herself, and land a second interview?

Dr. Joseph Johnston is a Professor of Counseling Psychology and the Director of the Career Center at the University of Missouri. He is familiar with situations like the one described above, and says, "It's important to know yourself well because even very bright people go bankrupt when it comes to explaining themselves." So how do you get to know yourself well? "Learning how to take a personal inventory is one of the many skills taught to our students at the career center," says Dr. Johnston.

Personal Inventory Overview

Taking a personal inventory is a skill that every college graduate needs to have. Therefore, this chapter is dedicated to helping you learn how to take your own personal inventory. Read the next couple of pages and then jot down your thoughts on the Personal Inventory Worksheet on page 31. There is no right or wrong way to do this, but to get the most out of your own personal inventory you are going to be required to ask yourself some tough questions. If you find this type of self-reflection difficult keep in mind that you don't have to do this all at one time. Coming back to it repeatedly over time can help you create a more complete profile.

The Grad to Great™ Personal Inventory was designed to help you find a career you'll love. Since you are most likely to excel at a career that optimizes both your strengths and your interests, the Grad to Great™ Personal Inventory consists of seven questions to help you identify the skills you enjoy using most.

Strengths and Weaknesses

You need to know what your strengths and weaknesses are. Can you give examples of each? If not, consider what supervisors, friends, and family members have said about you over the years. Ask your friends what your strengths are, but turn to your family for the truth about your weaknesses. Siblings will be especially happy to help you out in this particular area.

The following list is just a few examples to help you brainstorm your own list of strengths and weaknesses. For additional reading about how to explain your strengths and weaknesses to potential employers, we recommend *How to Say it at Work* by Jack Griffin (Prentice Hall, 1998).

Strengths

- Good motivator
- Able to block out distractions easily
- Highly organized
- Work well in teams
- Ability to adapt to changing needs of employer, or clients quickly
- Ability to acquire new skills quickly
- Creative
- Good problem solving skills

Weaknesses

- Procrastinator
- Perfectionist
- Impatient
- Uncomfortable speaking in front of groups
- Unable to work under pressure
- Hard time meeting deadlines
- Difficult to separate personal life from professional life
- Not punctual
- Unable to accept constructive criticism

An excellent book that can help you accurately pinpoint your strengths is *Now, Discover Your Strengths* by Marcus Buckingham and Donald O. Clifton (Simon & Schuster, 2001). When you purchase the book, you will receive a unique identification number that gives you access to their StrengthsFinder® Profile. The online test analyzes your basic reactions to multiple questions and then informs you of your five core strengths.

What do you think your strengths say about you? In what types of jobs do you think your strengths would be useful? Once you have identified your strengths, you need to be able to discuss several situations where your particular strengths were useful. Do not be vague. Say more than, "I helped in the vendor meeting." You need to tell stories like, "I pulled out the meeting notes from the previous year that clearly stated our request was in the scope of the project." The more you think about your strengths and learn to articulate them to others, the more likely you will be to make the most of an opportunity when it presents itself.

Keep in mind that everyone says they have "excellent people skills" but what does that really mean? To differentiate yourself from the crowd you have to explain which particular skills enable you to work well with people. Being able to give examples of how your strengths were useful in past situations is one way to outshine other applicants and win a job offer.

Now, consider your weaknesses. Knowing what your weaknesses are is important for several reasons. First, you should be aware of them for your own self-preservation. If there is something you know you are not great at, why say that you are? This does nothing but set you up to let others down. Second, by being aware of your own weaknesses you can seek out partnerships with people who are strong in the areas in which you need improvement. For example, if you have difficulty estimating the cost of a project, consult with someone who can give you some pointers and ask them to review the estimate before sending it out. Finally, knowing what your weaknesses are makes you more likely to recognize opportunities to improve them. For example, if you are not very organized and you can admit this, you will be more likely to read articles about organization and look for other ways to improve as well.

Do not confuse a weakness with something that you are simply not familiar with. Not knowing how to use a particular software program is not a weakness. An actual weakness is a particular skill that you lack or find especially challenging. For example, an inability to listen to others is a weakness. Review the sample list of strengths and weaknesses on page 19 to help you come up with your own list.

Some characteristics can be both strengths and weaknesses depending on how you present them. For example, someone who is impatient may tell an employer that is a weakness, while another job applicant may claim being impatient is what enables them to consistently complete projects on time. You should be aware of your own weaknesses and be realistic about whether it is a weakness that can be overcome. If it isn't, don't look for jobs that require that particular skill.

Table 2.1 Differences between Function, Field, and Industry

Function	Field	Industry
Accountant	Accounting	Hospitality (i.e. hotel)
Recruiter	Human Resources	Automotive
Marketing Coordinator	Marketing	Social Services (i.e. adoption agency)
Video Editor	Interactive Media	Communications
Professor	Economics	Education

What Are Your Transferable Skills?

A transferable skill is something you already do well. In your case, these are skills you acquired in college, but now wish to apply in a professional setting.

These skills are not specific to your major in school, or to the industry you wish to work in. In fact, transferable skills are independent of the environment in which they're used.

For example, let's say you are exceptionally resourceful. No matter what the problem is you can be depended on to find a solution. At school your resourcefulness helped you organize a major event. On vacation your resourcefulness enabled you to find and get a reservation at the trendiest restaurant. At your internship, your resourcefulness allowed you to put together a brilliant presentation for your boss. Resourcefulness is a transferable skill that most, if not all, employers would rate highly.

When you relate your transferable skills to an employer, identify the specific skill first, such as, "I am very resourceful." Then go one step further and think of an example of how being resourceful led to the successful completion of a project during an internship. This is how you articulate your transferable skills to an employer. Knowing how to do this will give you a significant edge over other job applicants.

Many recent graduates are unable to identify and articulate their transferable skills to a potential employer. When a potential employer asks what skills they bring to the work place, they cite specific skills related to the function for which they're applying. But since most recent graduates haven't worked long enough to possess the desired function-specific skills, they are unlikely to impress an employer with this type of answer. On the other hand, emphasizing your transferable skills can be a very effective way to impress an employer when you do not have any experience in your chosen field.

Think about your own transferable skills. Ask your friends and family what they think your transferable skills are. Articulating these skills is an incredibly powerful tool as you search for a job. Write these down when you think of them, and continue to do so throughout your career. You will be able to transfer many skills from one situation to the next as you progress professionally. To help you pinpoint your own transferrable skills, consider the examples in Table 2.2.

Table 2.2 Transferable Skills

Skills	Examples
Resourceful	Ability to locate hard to find information; handle difficult situations; or secure scarce resources.
Detail Oriented	Acute attention to minutia results in excellent follow-through on all projects and assignments.
Good Writer	Ability to prepare proposals, e-mails, speeches, newsletters, direct mail, letters, advertising copy, web site content, and interoffice memos.
Excellent Communicator	Ability to interact with clients, coworkers, and mangers in a meaningful way while maintaining a professional demeanor and keeping conflicts to a minimum.
Articulate	Ability to get a point across effectively and interact with clients, coworkers, and mangers in a professional manner.
Enthusiastic	Maintains a positive attitude towards challenges and obstacles. Ability to keep a team motivated.
Action Oriented	Determined to complete projects and assignments on time. Ability to focus on the task at hand and get the job done. Always ready to work.
Process Oriented	Avoids mistakes by carefully considering each project from all angles before starting any project. Meticulous planning results in very few unexpected delays and problems.

Skills	Examples
Strategic Thinker	Ability to prioritize effectively; separate issues into relevant "buckets"; anticipate potential challenges; and easily identify the most critical aspects of any project.
Organized	Reduces anxiety in the workplace due to ability to locate resources quickly and easily. Ability to develop new company processes in a methodical and well thought out manner that others can follow.
Excellent Public Speaker and Presenter	Exudes confidence in front of large groups and does not get rattled easily. Able to think on one's feet and stay focused on the subject matter. Ability to explain complex material in an easy to understand manner. Good teacher.
Good Listener	Ability to observe and read others. Quick to understand what someone is saying and able to follow directions.

What Can You Offer an Employer?

Do you know what you have to offer an employer? Can you explain how your contributions could play a role in the success of the company? Since you are unlikely to be able to offer ten years of experience in a particular field at this stage of your career, focus on translating what you know how to do into this new work environment. Talk about your transferable skills and the knowledge you have gained during school.

Along with your transferable skills, you also have the knowledge you acquired by majoring in a certain subject. But simply stating that you have a degree in your particular field is not helpful to an employer who is trying to decide how you fit into their company. Kelley Amadei, Regional Human Resources Manager of the Central United States for Heineken USA, says:

"You will do your career and your reputation a lot of good if you were to talk about the opportunities that you're looking for based more on the skill set that you've gained from your program, and based less on the title or just that you have the degree."

Your learning really begins after you graduate, and employers want to know that you understand this. You need to demonstrate to recruiters that not only can you do the job, but you are interested in learning too.

As you are brainstorming about your particular skill set don't overlook positive personality traits. Having a positive attitude and an upbeat disposition are often just as important to an employer as your technical skills. If you are a self-starter with desirable personality traits, you will move higher on a recruiter's list than candidates who have comparable technical skills, but who may not be as personable.

Building and retaining productive teams is critical to the profitability of any company. How are you going to add value to the particular team or division you'll work with? Recruiters and interviewers will ask you about this. They'll also ask you if you consider yourself a leader. Think about what experiences you've had working in teams and what experience you've had leading teams. What have you learned from these experiences? Be able to share examples that illustrate your ability to work well with others. You want to convince your potential employer that hiring you would be a good investment on their part.

What Kinds of Assignments Do You Enjoy?

What kind of assignments and projects would you enjoy doing? Kelley Amadei from Heineken USA mentioned that job seekers sometimes get so focused on the job title that they lose sight of what assignments the job will actually entail. Since the job description does not always accurately reflect the job, be sure to ask for specifics at the job interview. Knowing what assignments you'll be required to perform in the first few months lets you realistically assess if you would enjoy the position or not.

What are You Passionate About?

If you have a difficult time deciding what you want to do, think about your personal interests. What do you enjoy doing in your free time? What are your hobbies? Once you have compiled a list of what you enjoy, think about your

"Your degree doesn't define your life, just where you start. Don't be afraid to explore new fields, new directions, and new opportunities. When it's all said and done, let your epitaph be: 'They led a great life,' not 'They were a great employee.'"

Operations Manager
Age: 45
Denison University

future career. What jobs can you do that involve your hobbies?

We know of one young man who had a love of sailing and art. He found a job designing sails for a boating company when he graduated from college. The company hadn't advertised that particular position, but after seeing his art portfolio they hired him on the spot. What types of creative jobs can you come up with? If you can identify a need for the service you can provide, you'll be surprised how many companies are able to create a job just for you.

Remember, you don't have to know what you want to do for the rest of your life, but you should at least have a good idea about what you want to do in the next two years. During an interview many companies will ask you about your five-year plan and while some will argue that technology is rapidly destroying our ability to think in terms longer than six months, you'd better have an answer ready. It should be an answer that doesn't contradict anything else you've said during the job interview—but we'll get to interviews in Chapter 4.

What are Your Core Values?

Working for a company that has significantly different values from your own can be a challenge and one that is probably best avoided. To help identify your values ask yourself who the person in your life you most admire is, and why? What are the values that person holds dear? Chances are you have similar values.

One way to identify a company's values is to get on their web site and read about them. Look for their values and mission statements. You can also call the company and talk to people who work there. Talk to the alumni from your school who work there. Get their names from the online database if you have access, from the alumni relations office, or from the career center.

Now fill out the worksheet on page 31—remember looking at this more than once can be very useful, especially as your answers may change over time.

Back at the interview, Ellen decided to give Alyssa another chance. After taking the Grad to Great™ Personal Inventory, Alyssa was excited to answer Ellen's question again.

"Alyssa, if you had your choice, which division of our company would most interest you and why?"

This time Alyssa was ready. "I double majored in history and sociology. I feel that studying these subjects, in particular, has prepared me for a career in social science. Therefore, I would be very interested in joining a management consulting team that focuses on non-profits in developing markets."

Ellen smiled. Alyssa would definitely be getting an offer, she thought.

Now that you have given some thought to your own interests and ambitions, let's focus on the actual job search. In the next chapter you'll learn six things every grad needs to remember to do before the interview.

Chapter Summary

★ To impress employers you must be able to articulate who you are and what you want. You must be able to do this professionally and concisely.

★ Completing a personal inventory of your skills and interests is essential to your job search success. Be able to answer the following questions:

- What are my strengths?

- What are my weaknesses?

- What are my transferable skills?

- What can I offer an employer?

- What assignments would I enjoy?

- What am I passionate about?

- What are my core values?

★ Realize that learning doesn't stop when you graduate; it begins. Staying abreast of company procedures and the latest trends in your field is critical to career longevity.

★ My Personal Inventory Worksheet ★

What are my strengths?

_____

_____

What are my weaknesses?

_____

_____

What are my transferable skills?

_____

_____

What can I offer an employer?

_____

_____

What assignments would I enjoy?

_____

_____

What am I passionate about?

_____

_____

What are my core values?

_____

_____

SIX JOB SEARCH MUSTS

*"In any moment of decision,
the best thing you can do is the right thing;
the next best thing is the wrong thing;
and the worst thing you can do is nothing."*

Theodore Roosevelt

Getting your foot in the door isn't about saying what you think the employer wants to hear; it's about presenting your authentic self in the best possible light. This chapter explains six important things to remember when you're conducting a job search.

#1
Keep Your Online Image Clean

If you wouldn't want your mother to see it, keep it off the Internet. Employers are researching job applicants online in increasing numbers. According to a survey administered by the National Association of Colleges and Employers in 2006. Over a quarter of the organizations that responded to the survey reported having 'googled' or reviewed job applicant profiles on social networking sites such as Facebook or MySpace. While some employers expressed concern over the validity of information found online, others said they found this practice useful.

If you have a blog, podcast, web site—or you regularly participate on someone else's—be aware that what you put out there may be reviewed by a potential employer. Maintain a professional image both on and off the Internet and you won't have anything to worry about.

#2
Always Have an Updated Resumé

Keeping a well written, updated resumé handy is critical during your job search because this allows you take advantage of opportunities when you learn about them. For someone who wants to help you find a job there is nothing more frustrating than learning you don't have your resumé finished or updated. Even when you aren't looking for a job it is important to keep your resumé updated. Revisit your resumé at the end of each month to add new achievements and information.

While writing resumés is outside the scope of this book, there are many great resources that provide instruction on crafting a proper resumé.

"Pick where you want to live first, then find a job. The jobs will be there, trust me."

Logistics Manager
Age: 43
Western Kentucky University

#3
Know How to Write a Good Letter

The cover letter is your opportunity to really wow an employer. Make sure you address your letter to the person who should receive it. Large companies are likely to have highly structured recruiting procedures and policies. Your letter is unlikely to ever reach the hiring manager's desk if it is not addressed to them personally.

While knowing how to write a good cover letter is a must, you should also know how to write a really good plain old letter, and here's why. Suppose there is a company that you really want to work for, but they don't have any "open positions." Don't despair, simply write them a letter.

Anne landed job interviews simply by writing to two companies she wanted to work for. The letters were sent via e-mail. After both interviews she received job offers. And we have known several people who have either faxed, e-mailed, or snail mailed a letter to a company they wanted to work for and received positive results.

Do not feel limited to Internet job postings and career center listings. If there is something you are aching to do, write to the company. In our experience, this technique has proven to be more effective at smaller companies.

For your reference, we have included sample letters on pages 172–173.

#4
Never Miss an Opportunity to Network

This is so often an overlooked part of the job search, but finding a job through a friend of a friend is more convenient for you and for your potential employer. You come recommended so you'll probably be a good employee. Don't neglect to ask your network to recommend you for positions, or to suggest companies that might be a good fit.

To make the most out of networking opportunities, always carry business cards with you. Make sure your cards are professional in appearance and include an appropriate e-mail address. Cutesy or suggestive addresses are a turn-off to potential employers and networking contacts.

Who is in your personal network? If you think you don't have a network, you're not giving yourself enough credit. Your network includes teachers, members of your church, friends, family, people you play sports with, and anyone else with whom you have developed good rapport. Any one of these people could link you to your dream job. (See Chapter 8 for more about the benefits of networking.)

#5
Appreciate an Informational Interview

Too many job seekers blow informational interviews off as a waste of time, but they can be an invaluable resource. An informational interview is not a job interview. The purpose of a sit-down with a successful person is to learn from their experience, learn about their industry, and learn the steps that they took to get where they are. Informational interviews can be brief discussions over cups of coffee, formal meetings in an office setting, or anything in between.

We asked Amanda Nell, Director of Employer Relations at the University of Missouri to give us some tips on proper information interview etiquette.

★ When requesting an informational interview with someone, make sure to open with how you got their name. For example, "Professor Smith recommended I contact you regarding your experience in the natural energy industry." Personal references are always better than cold contacts.

★ Select someone in the position you wish to have someday, or who does almost exactly what you want to do. Ask them about their career path and how they got where they are today. Ask them for recommendations about how you can achieve your goals.

★ Ask them to look over your resumé and point out areas where you need improvement. This isn't about structural or grammatical improvements, but rather about your experience. Where are the gaps? Ask them to suggest things you could do to enhance your resumé. This is also an appropriate way to get your credentials in front of someone.

★ Do not ask for a job during an informational interview. There are a couple of reasons for this. First, they may not be aware of job openings at their company right now. Second, asking for a job is a yes or no question. You will lose out on the opportunity to learn about the career you are pursuing. Better they should be so impressed by you that they go and find out what positions are open and invite you to apply.

How exactly do you arrange to have an informational interview? There are no hard and fast rules, but one common method is to use your network. Who do you know that is in an industry in which you are interested? Do you have friends with a successful sibling or parent? Perhaps you have successful friends and you just want to sit down to pick their brain.

Even if you don't have a personal connection to someone, you can e-mail or telephone a complete stranger and state your interest in setting up an informational interview. Most times you will find people are flattered with your interest in them and more than willing to take time out of

"When I started my first job after college, I had no idea where my career would take me. I felt this immense pressure to choose the right career, the right job, the right company. I didn't understand that a "career" isn't about starting out on a set path that you'll follow for the next 30+ years. A career isn't set in stone and it isn't sedentary. I looked at my job as just that—a job—rather than as a development opportunity that would take me to the next step. Those that end up in careers that they love get there for a very specific reason— they took every opportunity to develop new skills; to discover their strengths; to try something new; and to identify the things that they really enjoy. More importantly, they never stopped planning; they never stood still."

Director of Alumni Relations
Age: 36
Undergrad University: Washington University

their schedule to meet you and talk about themselves. Since they are doing you a favor, be sure to meet at their convenience—and offer to pick up the check!

If you hit it off with your interviewee, they might know of someone else that you should talk to; they might know of a job that would be a good fit for you; and at the very least you just made a new contact in your network.

#6
Develop Your Own System for Rating Job Opportunities

The best way to stay focused during your job search is to develop your own rating system for jobs. Come up with three specific criteria that are must-haves for the position you will ultimately choose. An example of good criterion is, "I will be able to learn about TV advertising," as opposed to the more limiting, "I want to work for an advertising agency." You can get a lot of experience working in advertising for a company that is not an agency. This applies to most fields. Keep your options open.

Keep referring to your criteria to help you decide which opportunities will bring you closer to your goals. Some more examples of criteria for your rating system could be:

★ Location is near family

★ Location is nowhere near family

★ Salary is at least $35,000

★ The company promotes from within

★ The company provides training

★ I am allowed to make decisions on my own

★ I will learn how to write better articles

★ I will have access to the latest technologies

★ The company awards annual bonuses

★ The company will pay for relocation

★ I can specialize in my chosen field

Keep your list to three criteria that are most important to you. As you interview with different companies, think about how they stack up against your personal rating system. This is a way to prevent yourself from getting overwhelmed during your job search.

Now, you're ready to start preparing for your job interviews.

Chapter Summary

★ Since potential employers may conduct an Internet search for you, make sure you keep your online image professional. This applies to any web sites, forums, blogs, or networking sites to which you belong or participate.

★ Always keep your resumé updated so you can take advantage of opportunities when you learn about them.

★ Knowing how to write a good letter can help you gain entry to a company that isn't advertising open positions.

★ Since the majority of jobs are identified through personal contacts, don't neglect to take advantage of networking opportunities.

★ An informational interview is an opportunity to gather valuable information that you won't get in the classroom. Do not expect the person who has agreed to meet with you to offer you a job. Do realize that you will be in front of people who can recommend you to members of their network and help you expand your own.

★ Develop your own system to rate job offers. This allows you to make the best decision about which opportunity is right for you at this point in your career.

4

ACE ANY JOB INTERVIEW

*"Any fact facing us is not as important
as our attitude toward it,
for that determines our success or failure."*

Norman Vincent Peale

When you land a job interview you are halfway home, but to go all the way you must convince an employer that you are the best person for the job. In this chapter you'll learn why being authentic is the secret ingredient that can help you succeed in any interview situation and prove that you are the person they should hire.

There are a few key elements to a good interview—many of which you probably already know: arrive on time, dress appropriately, and have a good handshake. But what stands out—what really makes an impression on an employer—is your authenticity. Don't pretend you want to work in marketing if your heart truly lies in logistics, or vice versa. Employers can see through you when you answer questions how you think they want you to. If they *don't* see through you, you're in a worse position because you'll be considering a job you won't even enjoy.

Kelley Amadei, Regional Human Resources Manager of the Central United States for Heineken USA says:

"Be as authentic as you can be. I think a lot of graduates are trying to fit a mold. They shape the answers to their interview questions and their resumé based on what they think companies want to see. For me personally, whether it's been with Heineken or any other company, I want to see that person for who they are. Who they are in their personal life sometimes tells me more about who they are and what they're going to bring to the job force than any number of bullet points they're going to put on their resumé. So, when someone asks you what your strengths are, or what opportunities you are looking for, really spend some time before the interview reflecting on what you think they are, and not what you think the employer wants to hear. Really, do some self-reflection on what is going to make you happy, and if the job you are applying to is going to make you happy."

Remember the interviewer's opinion of you will be one of the deciding factors that determine if you get the job or not. You may only have an hour or less to impress them. It is their job to interview you, but it is up to you to ensure the interview goes smoothly. Also keep in mind you are interviewing them, too.

Don't Self-Select Out

Amanda Nell, Director of Employer Relations at the University of Missouri Career Center, revealed a shocking fact during an interview for this book. She said, "Many graduating seniors don't sign-up for on-campus interviews because they assume they are not qualified. They self-select out before they even try. It's a shame because they could be exactly what a job recruiter is looking for."

If you are still in college, go and sign up for on-campus interviews. Don't be intimidated by what the job description says. It is not your job to determine whether you are qualified for the job or not—that's the recruiter's job. Make them work. Don't pass up any opportunity to get in front of someone who could offer you a job you're interested in.

Do Your Homework

Research the company you are interviewing with. Make sure you have read everything on the web site. Check out Internet news sites. Look at the company's blog if they have one. Request a copy of their annual report if it isn't on the web site. The annual report will provide you with information about corporate strategy and the current direction of the company. You can also familiarize yourself with the faces of top executives and board members since their pictures are usually displayed in the annual report. Knowing who the top executives are may be useful if you are visiting the company and happen to run into one of them.

The interviewer may even ask you directly if you have done your homework on their company. If your answer is "no," that sends the message you are not prepared for the interview, or that you aren't that interested. Having done your research builds confidence. You will also be able to spend more time talking about you if you are able to spend less time having the interviewer give you background information on the company.

Don't neglect to find out in what type of setting the interview will take place. Most often you will meet in an office setting, but sometimes a recruiter will conduct an interview over a meal to observe your table manners. In jobs

---

Beth's Handshake Story

In Mrs. Kulpa's sixth grade class we had a career week. We had to select a profession, and I chose business management. She then held mock interviews and all students had to approach her one by one, introduce themselves, and shake her hand—just like on a real job interview.

After all the students had gone through the exercise, she called back only three students for a second mock interview. I still remember why she said we were called back—because we had a firm handshake and we looked her in eye while introducing ourselves.

I share this story because I have met many job hopefuls at recruiting fairs and a firm handshake definitely sets the tone and leads to a good first impression. Also, when shaking a woman's hand don't use a dainty handshake. When a man shakes my hand like that I am offended. In a business environment, shake hands like you mean it.

Careful not to squeeze their hand so hard as to almost crush their bones. A nice firm handshake is appropriate. Practice your handshake with someone you trust and get their feedback.

where you will be meeting with clients frequently, knowing proper etiquette is extremely important. If you are unfamiliar with table settings that include more than two forks you may wish to brush up on your etiquette.

Take Extra Copies of Your Resumé

Remember to take extra copies of your resumé to the interview. The person interviewing you may not have one, and if you are asked to meet with additional members of the staff, they may have not seen it. Decide how many extra copies to take based on the number of people that you expect to be interviewing with, and then add three. Make sure they are printed on nice paper.

Project Confidence

Walk confidently into the room or office and greet the person (or persons) who will be conducting the interview with a firm handshake. Do not hesitate or stop while crossing the room to shake hands since this will make you look nervous. Of course, if the person is sitting down and you have to wait for them to stand up, do so. The point is to appear confident.

Relax

When you're talking to the interviewer look them in the eye and be sure to smile. A good trick if you're nervous, or shy, is to pretend that the interviewer is an old friend. This will relax you and put a genuine smile on your face.

When you sit down, squeeze your buttocks together. This will make you sit up straight. It will also remind you to laugh at yourself a little, which, in turn, makes you appear more relaxed. Keep in mind that it is always best not to take yourself too seriously, because no one else is.

Interview dos and don'ts

★ Don't talk about personal issues

★ Don't bad mouth previous employers

★ Do lean forward to show interest

★ Do show an eagerness to learn

★ Do be able to describe a difficult work situation and what you learned from it

★ Do be able to describe a work project you excelled at

★ Do smile

★ Do demonstrate your ability to be flexible

★ Do be mindful of interview questions meant to weed you out

★ Do connect with your interviewer

★ Do keep your answers brief and to the point

★ Don't cross your arms—it's distracting or defensive

★ Don't ramble

★ Don't act like someone you're not, because even if you fool them you are unlikely to fit in once you start the job

★ Don't try to dazzle anyone with your experience if all you have on your resumé is an internship

★ Don't take off your shoes

★ Don't pick your nose

Over the years we have been on or participated in hundreds of job interviews and have kept an active list of the questions we have been asked. Here are a few you might come across on a first interview:

Sample Job Interview Questions

1. Tell me a little about yourself.

2. What is it about our company that makes you want to work here? Why did you apply?

3. What type of experience / qualifications do you have that relates to the position you are applying for?

4. What are your strengths?

5. What are your weaknesses?

6. What have been your greatest accomplishments recently?

7. What is the best compliment you have ever received in a work setting?

8. What is the biggest responsibility you have ever had at work?

9. What do you think about your boss?

10. What is the most challenging situation you have ever faced at work and how did you handle it?

11. What is the most important lesson you have ever learned?

12. What is important to you in a job?

13. What have you been doing since your last job?

14. What do you do on vacation?

15. I notice a gap on your resumé. What did you do for the six months you weren't working?

16. What qualities do you find important in a coworker?

17. Are you a good coworker to have? Why or why not?

18. Where do you see yourself in five years?

19. How do you define success?

20. What did you like the most about your last position?

21. Can you envision having your boss's job?

22. How does this position relate to your long-term goals?

23. What did you like the least about your previous position?

24. How does your previous experience relate to this position?

It's never a bad idea to practice your answers in front of a mirror or a friend before you go to the interview. Take advantage of the mock interviews offered by most career centers at your college or university. Doing so gives you an opportunity to figure out ahead of time which questions are most likely to trip you up.

Keep in mind that the person interviewing you may not have much experience conducting interviews. Make it your job to keep them at ease. This will take your mind off your own nerves. If they can't figure out what to ask you next, ask your own question, or offer to expand on your experience working with upset customers, for example. Just keep the conversation moving, and in a positive direction.

Beware of Questions Designed to Trip You Up

Christine, a senior executive at an investment bank, warns, "Some questions asked during the interview process are meant to kibosh you." Consider number 21 from the list of sample questions on page 50. What's the real meaning behind this question? The interviewer asks you this question to determine if you are ambitious and expect to be at your boss's level within a year. If this company wants ambitious entry-level workers, they want you to say yes. But what if their corporate culture does not encourage new hires to advance too quickly? Then the response more likely to get you hired would be, "Maybe in several years after I have gained enough experience." How can you know how to interpret the real meaning behind the interviewer's question? These tips were designed to help you get at the real meaning behind the question:

★ Determine whether it's a question that could be meant to "kibosh" you.

★ Listen to the tone of the person's voice.

★ Give a culturally appropriate answer for the company with which you are interviewing. (Do your homework ahead of time and during your informational interviews.)

★ Consider your tone of voice as you answer and think about what someone is likely to read into your tone.

Sally is a senior executive in Chicago. She advises to pay attention to the questions people ask you at a job interview because they say a lot about the company's corporate culture:

> "Several years ago I was interviewing with a major retail company and they asked me a series of questions that all related back to what my reaction would be if my coworkers were stealing. They asked me what I would do if my inventory logs got stolen, or even, I think, if my purse were to be stolen. At the time it didn't register, but guess what started to happen as soon as I started working there? My coworkers stole my inventory logs, and another colleague had her purse stolen. I later went to a different retail company and their questions were a stark contrast to my previous company. They asked me if I liked to make customers happy and if I genuinely liked people. It's funny, but both companies told me in one interview exactly what their values were."

Important Questions to Ask a Potential Employer

Now it's your turn to ask questions. To make a good impression at the interview, you should have a short list of questions memorized. To help get you started, we have included some questions for you to ask as well as some tips about what the answers may reveal.

1. **"What kind of qualities and skills would it take to really succeed and make a difference in this position?"**

   This question allows you to determine if you are a good match.

2. **"What would be the top priority of the person who accepts this job?"**

   You want to know if you would enjoy the tasks to which you will be assigned. For a variety of reasons, sometimes the job description does not accurately describe the job. Asking a few open ended questions about the specific duties you would be expected to perform can clarify this up front and save everyone a lot of time later down the road.

3. **"Can you describe a typical day for someone in this position?"**

   This will clarify the duties you will be asked to perform. If the tasks are a close match to those you identified on your personal inventory worksheet you should consider this job.

4. **"Why is this position available?"**

   You ask this question because you want to make sure that the boss isn't Meryl Streep's character from *The Devil Wears Prada*. You also want to make sure that you won't be set up to fail. If you receive an answer like, "We just haven't been able to find the right person yet and we've been through five hires in the past four months," that is a sign that something is not right with the management of the company. Drop that position from your list.

5. **"Was the person who previously held this position promoted? What is the usual progression for**

successful employees that have held this position previously?"

It's smart to be realistic about how likely you are to succeed in a specific position. If the company is well organized they will be prepared to help you succeed because replacing employees is expensive and time-consuming. If the interviewer says that no one who held the position previously ever moved up in the company, you may not want to pursue this job.

6. **"What are the most immediate challenges of the position that need to be addressed in the first six months?"**

You want to make sure that you will get to spend time working on assignments you will enjoy and find challenging. However, keep in mind that no one gets to start out at the top. There will be tasks you do not enjoy, but doing them well will ensure you are assigned more interesting work.

7. **"What are the performance expectations of this position and what is the evaluation process?"**

For many recent graduates a lack of feedback can be a real shock to the system. In the working world your boss is unlikely to stop by your desk every day to tell you what a wonderful job you are doing. At some offices, the only time you may receive any feedback is during a midyear or end of the year review. Some smaller companies do not even have performance reviews. This is a good question to ask so you know what to expect and you can decide if that type of process will work for you.

8. **"What challenges might I encounter if I take this job?"**

This lets the interviewer know that you realize no job is perfect and that you are willing to face the challenges ahead of you. The answer may also tip you off about a bad-tempered boss, financial difficulties within the company, or issues with the building facilities where you may be working. Get as much information as possible so you can make the best decision.

9. **"How would you describe your management style?"**

If the person interviewing you will also be your boss, now is the best time to find out if you would enjoy working for them. The relationship you have with your boss will be an important one. This is a person that can help you on your journey to career success. This is also a person that can make you work so much overtime you won't remember your significant other's name. It's always a good idea to try to find out what you're getting into.

10. Ask a question or two specific to the company you are interviewing with. For example, "I read in the annual report that you are going to be outsourcing software development projects overseas starting this year. Are there any opportunities to work on these initiatives at the level at which I would be starting out?"

Ask a question that shows you have done your homework on their company. Don't just ask the generic questions about the particular position for which you are applying. Show an interest in the company's vision. Ask questions that provide information about which areas interest you most.

11. "What are the next steps in the interview process?"

This is a great question to close with. If at the end of the interview you are definitely interested in the position, say so. For example, "I am excited about what I've learned today, and I am even more interested in the position now after speaking with you. What are our next steps?" This is a compliment to the interviewer—getting you excited about the company means they've done their job. You also give the right kind of immediate response. They now know you will come back for a second interview if asked.

Follow-Up

After a job interview, make sure you follow up. It is important to prove you are thorough right from the beginning. Treat the application process as if it were your full-time job.

Some companies won't hire you unless they receive a thank you letter following the interview. Send a thank you note not only to those who have interviewed you, but to anyone who has helped you during your job search. While e-mail is now acceptable, you will make a better impression on your contacts if you send a handwritten note on appropriate stationery. For job interviews, you might prefer the immediacy of e-mail. You may get a sense of which format your interviewer would prefer during the interview. Including a mention of something positive you talked about in your thank you note is a good way to re-mind the recipient which candidate you were.

If you have trouble writing thank you letters, check out the web site www.thank-you-note-samples.com for some free advice. Kathy—who runs the web site—offers some great pointers for writing thank you letters, and she might even write one for you for free. Though if she does, you better send her a nice thank you note.

If you haven't heard from your interviewer during the timeframe promised, follow up with a phone call. If you are directed to voicemail, leave a brief message explaining you are just following up and checking to see if they needed any more information from you. Reiterate your interest in the position and close by stating you look for-ward to hearing from them.

If you are turned down for the job, it is perfectly reason-able for you to call the interviewer and ask for some feed-back. This must be done courteously and with the true in-tention of learning what you can improve for the future. Do not call to argue with them. They have made their deci-sion and you are not going to change their mind. Simply

> "If your company is in the middle of a strike when you start your first day, it may be a sign it's not a place where you want to grow a career."
>
> Strategy Director
> Age: 30
> University of Michigan

state your request for comments to develop a better understanding of how you come off during interviews. For example:

"Hello, Mr. Interviewer. I understand you have already made a decision about the marketing position. However, I was hoping you might be able to give me some feedback on how I could improve during the interview process in the future. I am still very interested in pursuing a position similar to the one for which I interviewed with you, and really want to learn what I can do better."

This is non-confrontational and lets the interviewer know you are not calling to vent your frustrations. If the interviewer does take the time to speak with you—some will, some won't—be sure to thank them for their time. This type of feedback will be invaluable. Who knows, you may even learn that you were their first choice, but they were forced to hire the boss's kid.

Chapter Summary

★ Be authentic if you want to impress a potential employer.

★ If you're unsure if you're qualified for a certain job, apply and interview anyway. Never self-select out of a potential opportunity to be offered a job.

★ Research the company and find out what the format will be ahead of time.

★ Take extra copies of your resumé.

★ Speak and walk with confidence. The company may need you more than you need them.

★ You want to appear relaxed. Employers don't want to hire someone that is uptight or nervous.

★ Practice your answers to questions employers are likely to ask you.

★ Be aware of questions designed to weed you out.

★ Ask the interviewer your own questions. These should be about the company, not about salary or vacation time. Save those questions for the second interview.

★ Follow-up after your interview with a thank you note, and phone call if necessary.

5

TEN MISTAKES TO AVOID AT WORK

"There is a way to do it better...find it."

Thomas Edison

There are ten common mistakes you are likely to make when you are just starting out in your first career. In this chapter you'll learn what those mistakes are and how to avoid them.

#1
Not Asking for Help

When you land that first job, of course you want to make a good impression, but there is a difference between wanting to make a good impression and just flat out wanting to impress everyone. A sign that you are more concerned with the latter is if you find yourself reluctant to ask for help when you need it.

Keep in mind that asking for help is not a sign of weakness, or even inexperience. To the contrary, it is a sign of maturity and will send a signal to your boss that you can be trusted to speak up when you are in trouble. Ultimately, this will inspire confidence in your abilities and you'll soon find your peers coming to you for answers to the questions they were too scared to ask.

Often people are afraid to ask for help out of fear that others will think less of their capabilities. While researching work environments for this book, we interviewed several professionals and their supervisors about this topic. A computer programmer from Chicago said, "I don't like asking for help because I don't want to give the impression that I need to be micromanaged." We found this to be a concern among many of the young professionals we spoke with.

The manager of this man shared a different viewpoint. She said, "I would be much less likely to worry that I need to prioritize his time if he would simply tell me ahead of time where he needs help. I want him to come to me for help. That's what I'm here for. If he didn't need my help he'd be doing my job."

People expect you to need some help along the way, and you will be much better off asking for help as soon as you realize you need it.

Anne's Adventures in TV

At 22 I was working as a television news producer in Santa Barbara, California. I was responsible for writing the news stories, deciding in which order they would be read by the anchor during the broadcast, supervising staff, printing scripts, and timing everything on air. I had been producing television news in Michigan since I was 19 and had received excellent performance reviews and ratings. I was on my way to a brilliant career in broadcasting (or so I thought).

When I arrived in Santa Barbara, I felt I knew everything about producing the news. I was expecting a call from Tom Brokaw any day. However, I was having one teensy tiny problem. I could not get the ink jet printer to work that printed off the anchors' scripts. It was a completely different setup than the one I had been trained on at my previous station. It was the most confusing machine I had ever seen, but I did not want to ask anyone for help with something so trivial. Since I refused to admit I needed help, every time we went on air for the 5 p.m. and 11 p.m. news, the anchors ended up at the news desk with no scripts. Anchors do not like going on air without scripts. Without scripts, if the teleprompter stops working, anchors have no idea what to say. Unfortunately, at this station the teleprompter went dead a lot. In fact, in the summer of 1998, several thousand residents of California faithfully tuned in to the weekend news only to find an attractive anchorwoman staring back at them with a slightly bitter expression on her face.

It probably seems silly to you that I wouldn't just ask someone to show me how to use the script printer. It seems silly to me now too! At the time I felt that would be admitting that I wasn't experienced enough to do my job. If I had just admitted that I didn't know how to load the news stories into the printer fast enough to allow enough time for the scripts to be ready, I am sure my boss would have been happy to help me. Instead, whenever anyone asked when the scripts would be ready I got defensive and told them I had it under control and to mind their own business.

It was a mess, newscast after newscast, and eventually I was fired. The kicker is that I wasn't even fired for sending the anchors on air without scripts. I was fired because I didn't ask for help. My boss said, "If I can't trust you to come to me for help when you need it, how can I trust you to accurately report the news to our viewers?

Never be afraid to ask for help. Employers expect new hires to have questions, and they count on you to speak up and ask them. No one can read your mind and they shouldn't have to. It is your responsibility to make sure that you request clarification for anything that is unclear to you. If you feel that you need more training to better perform your current duties, consider the following:

★ Could you benefit from simply reading more about your particular function or industry?

★ Does your company have a policy for employee training programs?

★ Are there any organizations you could join that would help you improve your job performance?

★ Can you ask your boss if you can sit in on meetings where you can learn more about the company and general business practices?

Conversely, if you are able to offer help to a coworker or manager, do so without hesitation.

#2
Trying to Show Up Your Boss

Some people believe that to be a star at work they must outshine their boss. These folks may contradict their boss in meetings, or otherwise go to great lengths to point out inefficiencies in a boss's set of standard operating procedures. This is a really bad idea. Constantly trying to show up your boss is one of the biggest mistakes you can make, and not just at the beginning of your career. Some people never learn this rule and are flabbergasted each time they're turned down for a promotion.

You don't want to compete with your boss. You have a lot to learn from them, and it's in your best interest to make them look good. They can be your champion and are in the best position to put in a good word about you to the higher-ups. They can recommend you for bonuses, raises, and even promotions. If you get off on the wrong foot, or are suspected of feelings of misguided superiority, your boss can and will stand in the way of all promotions, raises, and approved vacation time. They may even fire you. As a new hire you are unproven, and you have very little leverage against someone who may have been with the company for years. Concentrate on doing your best work, not pointing out the flaws of others.

#3
Not Showing Up On Time

This seems rather straightforward, doesn't it? You are either on time or you are late. Nothing more really needs to be said, right? Good, moving on...

...but wait; why then does getting to work on time pose such an insurmountable challenge for so many people? Furthermore, why are some people fired immediately for this trespass while others are allowed to stroll in whenever they want with no consequence whatsoever?

We have a few theories. Before getting into them, let us say this: It is always best to get to work on time. If you are supposed to start at 8 a.m. then you need to be at work at that time or earlier. It doesn't matter if you are an actor, a waiter, a business professional, or a kayaking instructor—you need to be at your set, station, cubicle, or beach at the designated time.

Being on time is not only expected in the morning (or whenever you start your shift). You must arrive on time for all meetings and appointments too. This is especially true for new hires. Your company hasn't yet had an opportunity to see what you're capable of. Not showing up on time makes a bad impression, and one that will be hard to shake.

Your employer depends on you to show up on time, and they trust you will do so without having to be constantly reminded. While there is no penalty for showing up early, you could get fired for showing up late. By showing up a few minutes early you give yourself time to get caught up on e-mails and voicemails. You can use the time to brainstorm ideas and write them in a notebook that you keep in your desk. You'll decrease your stress level and minimize the chance of getting trapped in traffic or missing your bus.

While every work environment is unique, there is one universal rule—face time. If your boss sees you doing a great job, they think you are a good employee. If they don't see you, they wonder where the heck you are. Worse, they don't think about you at all. It's like the phrase, "Out of sight, out of mind." If you are not in plain sight of your superiors, you are not on their radar. If you are not on the radar, you are definitely not at the top of the list for a promotion. People who get a lot of face time with the boss and make a positive impression, are less likely to get fired, even if they show up late once in a while. People who don't interface with the boss often and show up late, are more likely to be let go.

If you are coming in late more often than you should be, consider your level of interest in your work. Are you challenged? Do you enjoy your job? If not, you may want to think of ways to make your position more challenging.

If you think you are experiencing serious burnout, then you may wish to start looking elsewhere. But if you do still enjoy your job and just can't stop hitting the snooze button, suck it up. Go to bed earlier. Get your butt to work on time before others start assuming you simply don't care anymore.

If you are consistently showing up to work late because of outside responsibilities, like raising children or caring for an elderly person, discuss your situation with your boss. You may be surprised how willing they are to work with you to find a solution. Perhaps you will even be offered the opportunity to change your work hours to accommodate your other responsibilities. Don't expect this, but it has been known to happen.

#4
Not Learning From Your Coworkers

Sometimes the information you need is only a desk away. People have all kinds of experience and you can learn something from everyone. Why lose out on an opportunity to learn from those closest to you, like friends, family, and...coworkers.

Unfortunately, these opportunities are often overlooked due to competitive work environments or personal insecurities. Instead of looking at your colleagues as competitors for the next promotion, try to look for ways to build professional relationships with the coworkers you admire, and learn as much as you can from them. Be willing to share your knowledge as well. You never know—the insights you share may help transform someone's attitude, career, or life. Developing good relationships with your coworkers also creates a more enjoyable workplace.

"I wish I would have asked more questions. Asking questions ensures that the right thing is being done and engages other people."

Interim Manager Surgical ICU
Age: 31
Vanderbilt University

#5
Being Afraid to Make Mistakes

Let's face it: everybody makes mistakes at work. It's inevitable. If you plan to work for more than a day over the course of your lifetime, you are going to make a mistake at some point. You don't want to be so scared to make a mistake that you're paralyzed at work. The only mistake you should worry about is the one you repeat. If you can view your mistakes as learning experiences and move on you'll be fine. You have to show initiative at work in order to make a good impression and have an impact. You can't do that if you're too worried about messing up.

In addition, fear of mistakes may cause you to "play it safe" all the time. When this happens, your managers assume that you are not going to step up and be a leader. They see you as someone who is too scared to take a risk and not a person that is able to think "out of the box." You will not be asked to head up any important initiatives at work and you definitely won't be promoted.

#6
Not Admitting You've Made a Mistake

This one can really come back to haunt you. If someone else discovers your mistake and outs you, you will look incompetent—or worse—dishonest. The best policy is to admit a mistake right away and offer up a solution to fix it immediately. People make mistakes. Don't beat yourself up about it. Accept responsibility for your mistake, fix it, and move on.

#7
Not Being Able to Handle Feedback

The authors would like to applaud Generation Y, or the Millennials (born 1980–1995), for shaking up the working world regarding feedback. By demanding more timely feedback from managers, Gen Y is forcing human resource departments to reconsider their formal employee evaluation processes.

Standard practice in most companies—including many we've worked for—is annual performance evaluations. A manager rates an employee using whatever system the company has developed. The employee is given the opportunity to review the document and make comments of their own. The manager and employee then meet to discuss the evaluation and make a decision about an increase in salary. And that's it: a discussion about your performance once a year.

Fortunately, this is starting to change now that Gen Y is entering the workforce in such large numbers. Companies are realizing they cannot ignore the needs of the Millennials without risking a shortage of talent. Increasingly companies are now coaching their managers on ways to give more timely feedback.

We're not saying you should expect your manager to comment on every little task you're doing right or wrong. It's likely the comments you receive will be more subtle. When you sit down with your manager for your annual performance evaluation, you are receiving formal feedback. This will be documented and placed in your personnel file. But, we're talking about informal feedback. This is the type of feedback that you are receiving on a daily basis from coworkers, clients, managers, and even your family and friends.

Informal feedback is delivered to you through another person's body language, subtle comments, or directly. To benefit from informal feedback you must have self-awareness and learn to pick up on the signals that are others are sending to you.

Now that companies are aware that employees want frequent feedback, and now that you can recognize the signs of informal feedback, can you handle all of it? It is important that you develop the ability to handle feedback that may be difficult to hear—in other words—criticism.

If someone is willing to provide feedback to you directly, be grateful. Realize that in most circumstances it is harder for the person to offer the criticism than it is for you to hear it. Most people do not want to intentionally hurt your feelings or make you feel bad about yourself. People who take the time to offer you constructive criticism do so because they see potential in you and they want to nurture that potential.

The worst thing you can do is to get defensive and shut down. This will make the person who is trying to help you back off. They'll realize you can't handle this type of feedback, and they will stop trying to help you. If you are getting emotionally overloaded with what you are hearing, simply say, "Thank you. I hear what you're saying, but I need some time to digest all of this." You can always go back to the person later and ask some clarifying questions.

#8
Having a Bad Attitude

Besides making you a miserable person, a bad attitude is going to make you very unpopular with your coworkers. You may not be trying to win a popularity contest, but getting along with coworkers is crucial to your success. Colleagues can help give your ideas and initiatives momentum. They can pick you up on a rough day. If you don't want to alienate your colleagues it is vital to have a positive attitude at work.

Having a bad attitude is draining mentally. It's exhausting to be in a negative frame of mind all the time. Chances are you have been described as someone with a bad attitude if you:

- Are inflexible

- Tend to believe people are out to take advantage of you

- Talk about people behind their backs instead of talking to them directly

- Think that no one gives you enough credit and believe the company would be better off if everyone would just listen to you

- Always point out reasons why people or projects are destined to fail

- Criticize everything that your company does or doesn't do

- Do not realize that your depressing commentary on everything drains the energy of everyone around you

People understand you have days when you are not at your best. But there's a difference between having a few bad days out of 365 as opposed to only a few good days. To keep your spirits high, try meditation or take out your frustrations during a kickboxing class before or after work. The endorphins released during exercise can help keep you in a good mood all day long.

#9
Engaging in Office Gossip

Hopefully you aren't the office gossip. Too much focus on what others are doing means less time to focus on your own job performance. What others do is not your primary concern. Focus on you and your job.

That being said, we realize there may be times when you are forced to listen to office gossip. For example, if the CEO walks into your office and starts talking about your co-worker who keeps showing up late, you probably don't want to interrupt with, "I'm sorry Mr. CEO, but I don't listen to gossip." Go ahead and listen, but don't under any circumstance repeat what you have heard. Especially because if it gets back to the CEO that you told people what he said, guess who he's likely to be bad-mouthing next? Additionally, don't take it upon yourself to tell the CEO what you think about your coworker because then you become the office gossip.

An especially precarious situation is created the moment someone asks you, "What do you think about so-and-so?"

When Tina was working for a brokerage firm in her early career, she was walking down the hallway when a coworker named Cindy, who was leaving to go on a Mexican vacation the next day, stopped her to chat. Not too long after they had started talking Cindy asked, "So, Tina, what do you think about Ralph?"

Tina worked with Ralph a lot. She relied on him to get good rates for her clients and he was always helpful in that capacity. But Tina didn't really like Ralph all that much. Tina replied, "Ralph? Well, actually I think he's loud, obnoxious, and kind of a sleaze-bag."

A few weeks later Tina saw Ralph in the cafeteria. She noticed he was quite tanned. She waved hello, but Ralph turned around and ignored her. Assuming he hadn't seen her, Tina turned to another coworker, Sam, who was behind her in line and mused, "Ralph's awfully tanned. I wonder where he went?"

Sam replied, "Mexico."

"Oh really? What a coincidence! Cindy just went to Mexico too."

"Yes I know. They shared a room," Sam said.

Ouch! You can imagine the level of service Tina received from Ralph after that. After that experience, Tina advises that if someone asks your opinion about anyone in the office, answer as if the person in question is a close relative of the person who's doing the asking.

#10
Not Understanding Generational Differences

Today there are four generations working side by side in most companies, and each group has different ideas about the most effective way to get work accomplished. Not understanding the differences between these generations is a big mistake. You will have a much easier time working with people from other generations if you recognize what is most important to them and understand where their attitudes towards their work originates. Doing so will set you apart from your peers.

Depending on which source you reference, the generations may be categorized slightly differently, but throughout this book we will refer to the following:

- **Matures (born 1901–1945)**

- **Baby Boomers (born 1946–1964)**

- **Generation X (born 1965–1978)**

- **Generation Y/ Millennials (born 1979–1988)**

People from the same generation share a certain type of bond whether they even like each other or not. They share common experiences rooted in the world events that took place during their youth. Their reactions to these events helped to shape their values, and these values shape their attitudes towards their work.

The economic, political, and social events that occurred while you were growing up had an impact on how you view the world today. Think about your great-grandmother telling you stories of how she rationed food during WWII. Or how her father grew up during the depression and lost all the money he had in the bank, and from then on kept all his money hidden around the house. Events such as the Great Depression and World War II had lasting effects on the generations that grew up during that time. Can you even imagine stashing all of your money in your house and not in a bank? Every Baby Boomer can recall what they were doing when they first heard that John

Table 5.1

Experiences and life events that shaped each generation	
Matures (born 1901–1945)	**Baby Boomers (1946–1964)**
• Great Depression • WWII / Korean Wars • New Deal • Rise of Labor Unions • One Company Career	• Civil Rights • Sexual Revolution / The Pill • John F. Kennedy Assassination • Woodstock / Watergate • Cold War • Moon Landing
Generation X (1965–1978)	**Generation Y/ Millennials (1979–1988)**
• Challenger Explosion • Fall of Berlin Wall / Fall of Communism • Personal / classroom computer • Two Career Parents Latchkey Kids • AIDS • Desert Storm • Corporate Downsizing • Missing children on milk cartons	• School shootings • Oklahoma City Bombing • Child focused world • Team emphasis in Education • Clinton / Lewinsky Scandal • Growth of the Internet / Digital Age • Reality TV • Attacks of 9/11 • Corporate & Government Scandals

F. Kennedy was assassinated. Gen X remembers what they were doing when the Challenger exploded. Of course for Millennials the touchstone is September 11, 2001.

Can you relate to the following?

- Nathan, a 23-year-old, fresh college grad, is eager to set his career on fire. "I'm going to be CEO by the time I'm 30," he announces to his older colleagues on his first day, annoying them immediately.

- Emily, a 29-year-old consultant, cringes under her managers' leadership style. "If she doesn't stop micromanaging me and let me do it my way, I'm totally out of here," she thinks.

- Jeff, a 32-year old purchasing manager, can't get over the long hours his 52-year old boss puts in. "Its only a job" he thinks.

- Bianca, a 46-year-old mother of three and caretaker for her elderly father looks at the upcoming election and wonders how she'll ever find the time to meet the needs of both her family and the campaign team. She also wonders if her hard work and loyalty over the past 25 years will be enough to keep her as a highly thought of employee if she has to take off time during this election?

- George, a 62-year-old employee with 35 years at the company, sits back and observes the new crew of college grads settle into their positions at his company. He can't believe that these kids don't have more respect or loyalty for his company; at their age he was happy to have a job.

- Belinda, a 24-year-old, marketing analyst with one year experience, suggests an idea to her 47-year-old boss, Sam. Sam replies with "We tried that in 1992, don't you have any new ideas?"

Table 5.2 was compiled from research conducted by Cam Marston, author of *Motivating the "What's in it for Me?" Workforce* (John Wiley & Sons, 2007) and illustrates common attitudes each generation brings to the workplace.

With this much diversity in the age of workers it is important to understand how each generation communicates. Communication is the key to bridge the generation gap. Research has shown that Matures appreciate straightforward messages, while Boomers prefer quick and to the point communication. Gen Xer's like to be communicated with frequently, and Millennials want personalized communication and positive reinforcement from their boss.

When working with more senior coworkers who might not have the same technological skills you have, be willing to teach and learn from them. Remember they didn't grow up with the same technology you did. They are no less intelligent than you, they just aren't as familiar the newer computer programs. If you were suddenly required to use shorthand at work instead of a word processor you might not come off looking so smart. Be patient and don't talk down to colleagues who might have used their first computer at work just a few years ago. Older colleagues might be defensive and patronizing because they are intimidated and worry the younger crop of workers will take their jobs. Look for ways to partner with them instead of aggravate them. Be willing to listen as opposed to trying to impress everyone all the time.

Table 5.2

Generations in the Workplace	
Matures (born 1901–1945) • Loyal to employer and expect the same in return. • Superb interpersonal skills. • Enjoying flextime arrangements today so they can work on their own schedule. • Believe promotions, raises, and recognition should come from job tenure. • Measure work ethic on timeliness, productivity, and not drawing attention.	**Baby Boomers (1946–1964)** • Believe in, champion, and evaluate themselves and others based on their work ethic. • Work ethic measured in hours worked. Productivity is less important. • Believe teamwork is critical to success. • Believe relationship building is very important. • Expect loyalty from those they work with.
Generation X (1965–1978) • Eschew the hard-core, super-motivated, do or die Boomer work ethic. • Want open communication regardless of position, title, or tenure. • Respect production over tenure. • Value control of their time. • Look for a person to whom they can invest loyalty, not a company.	**Generation Y/ Millennials (1979–1988)** • Searching for individuals who will help them achieve their goals. • Want open, constant communication and positive reinforcement from boss. • Find working with someone of the Mature generation easy to do. • Searching for a job that provides great, personal fulfillment and ways to shed the stress in their lives.

Reprinted with permission from Cam Marston, Marston Communications
www.marstoncomm.com

Let older managers know that you understand they have more strategic skills than you do at this point. They do. Keep in mind that using a computer to get your job done is different from being able to identify what the job is that needs to get done. In most cases, the company was doing fine before you got there; be respectful of the people who came before you and paved the way. Think about how you'll expect to be treated ten to twenty years from now.

Now that you have more information about the generations, lets revisit the scenarios from earlier:

- Nathan is the 23-year-old who's eager to let his colleagues know of his intentions to be CEO by the time he's 30. While admirable, informing everyone of his ambition is not the way to go. Nathan would be better served by discussing his desire for rapid advancement privately with his boss. Seeking a mentor, and having a good relationship with his boss will allow him to gain extra assignments and get noticed by the top executives. Nathan also needs to learn that if he is to become a manger, his colleagues will not be out to sabotage him if he treats them with respect and champions their ideas along with his own. A leader is only effective if the people follow. If Nathan continues to act pompous, his colleagues may band together and render him entirely ineffective by cutting him out of important projects and decisions.

- Emily, the 29-year-old consultant who can't stand being micromanaged, needs to get proactive. First, she needs to explore why she feels she is being micromanaged. Being questioned on assignments, or being asked to redo something, is not necessarily micromanagement. It could just be part of the learning curve each employee goes through when they work for someone new. Second, Emily must determine whether she is truly being micromanaged, or just feeling defensive. If ultimately Emily comes to the conclusion that she is being micromanaged, she will need to confront her boss. Micromanagement is often a work style exhibited by a boss who has trouble delegating work. For a variety of reasons they would rather do the work themselves then have someone else do it. (See Chapter 9 for more about dealing with micromanagers.)

- Jeff is the 32-year old purchasing manager who can't get over the long hours his baby boomer boss puts in. Jeff needs to realize this is a generational difference and that his quality of work is not defined by the number of hours he puts in. Once this sinks in he will feel confident about setting boundaries concerning the amount of overtime he works. Jeff's boss will respect him as long as he gets his work done right, and on time.

- Bianca is the 46-year-old mother of three and caretaker for her elderly father who is worried about balancing her personal responsibilities with her job. The best thing she can do is to prioritize her time. With the election coming up she can telecommute from home so she will be in both places if necessary. She will have to rely on her campaign team to pull their weight, and realize that her dedication is not measured in the number of hours she puts in, but rather in the quality of work.

- George is the 62-year-old employee with 35 years at the company who can't believe the lack of loyalty from new crew of college grads. George would be much better off talking to these new employees than rushing to judgment about their loyalty to the company. He could also learn a few tricks from these employees to make his job more efficient, while also mentoring these new hires at the same time. Loyalty to a company is much different today, than it was thirty years ago. Today's young employees might only stay at a particular company for two to three years, but they will work hard while they're there.

- Belinda is the 24-year-old, marketing analyst with one year of experience who suggested an idea to her 47-year-old boss, Sam, who discounted the idea immediately because it was attempted back in 1992. Belinda shouldn't get discouraged or develop a bad attitude. This is Sam's problem, not hers. Sam would be much more successful with his new employees if he wasn't so apt to recount the past and discourage his new employees from suggesting ideas. Belinda needs to continue thinking of new ideas and bringing them forward for implementation. Eventually management will see she's a self-starter and she may end up as Sam's boss.

Chapter Summary

★ Ask for help when you need it.

★ Do not try to make your boss look bad.

★ Always get to work on time and remember, early is on time.

★ Look for ways to learn something new from your coworkers.

★ Don't be afraid to make mistakes. They are a good way to learn something you aren't likely to forget.

★ If you make a mistake, admit it.

★ Appreciate constructive criticism and use such feedback to improve your job performance.

★ Maintain a positive attitude at work. Blow off steam at the gym before or after work. Try meditation.

★ Don't gossip. Listen if you have to, but don't repeat anything.

★ Understanding the generational differences in the work place can help your interpersonal skills in the office and give you an edge over your colleagues.

6

GETTING PEOPLE TO LISTEN TO YOU

"The greatest compliment that was ever paid me was when someone asked me what I thought, and attended to my answer."

Henry David Thoreau

If you want people to buy into your ideas, you need to get them to buy into you first. To do that you need to have credibility and you need to have demonstrated competence. This chapter teaches you how to persuade others to buy in to you so your ideas will be heard.

Jan D'Arcy is an executive speech coach with over thirty years of experience assisting C-level executives, scientists, and NASA engineers to become effective communicators. At one point in her career she surveyed 300 professionals to find the shared traits among model communicators. One question on her survey asked respondents who they would be compelled to listen to at work.

Two answers were given consistently:

- Someone who has gained my TRUST (credibility)
- Someone with EXPERIENCE in the trenches (competence)

If you can demonstrate that you are trustworthy and that you know what you're talking about, people will listen to you.

Credibility and Competence

Think about the last courtroom drama you watched on television. Odds are there was at least one scene in which an attorney attempted to discredit a witness. Perhaps, for effect, that scene was preceded by a montage of the attorneys racing around the city gathering background information (aka dirt) on the witness. You watch the lawyers exert tremendous effort searching for something in the witness's past—something to prove he cannot be trusted. When that silver bullet is finally discovered the attorneys are elated. The courtroom scene reaches its climax as the judge orders the jury to discount the testimony of the witness. The attorneys have proved he cannot be trusted and therefore, he is not a credible witness. His entire testimony must be thrown out.

Credibility equals trust in the mindset of most people. So in order to get people to listen to you at work, you must first persuade them to trust you. No matter if you work as a teacher, a scientist or the president of the United States, people won't listen to you if they don't trust you. You do not have credibility until you prove you are trustworthy.

Think about someone you do not altogether trust. Picture this person carefully in your mind. How much stock do you put in what they have to say? Probably not much.

People have to *want* to listen to you. Otherwise they simply won't care about what you have to say. If you have someone's trust—if you have credibility—they have an incentive to listen.

When you are the new kid on the block—the new hire—it can be a challenge to build credibility with your managers and peers. Fortunately there is plenty you can do to get your new workmates to buy into you.

During an interview for this book, Executive Speech Coach Jan D'Arcy introduced the concept of "unique insight." Realize that even though you do not have the experience yet, you do have unique insight. This insight is derived from all the experiences you have had in your life to this point. Think about what you can do well and what skills you have that can be transferred to the job at hand. Trust in your skills, and in your own self. Use your unique insight to propel you forward. This is an especially useful concept to use in any situation where you need to build credibility.

The concept of unique insight also relates to authenticity—a concept we discussed in Chapters 2 and 4. By drawing upon your own experiences to make observations and offer commentary in the workplace, you guarantee the integrity of what you say. This is simply because you use your own experience. People are more likely to trust you when you talk about something you have actually seen, touched, or heard firsthand.

Now let's explore the importance of competence. No one wants to listen to someone who doesn't know what they're doing: you need to be competent. How do you pass yourself off as competent when you do not have much, if any, experience? We asked Jan this during our interview.

"How do you learn to be competent? You do! You need to put what you have learned into action. Take advantage of every opportunity that comes your way to get hands-on experience. Being competent is more than understanding. You can have an understanding of something, but you are not competent at something until you actually do it. You become competent by stretching your understanding into action. You can't fake competence and you can't fake experience."

To build your competence she suggests these five action steps:

- ★ Find a mentor
- ★ Develop relationships
- ★ Get on committees
- ★ Volunteer for assignments
- ★ Volunteer to go to conferences

These are five ways you can immerse yourself in your subject matter or area of expertise at work. You further immerse yourself in your new field by surrounding yourself with people that work in your area and absorbing as much information as you can. Learn as much as you can from them and from any trade magazines, websites, or other resources that you can find. Apply your knowledge by getting hands-on experience in your field. Jan explains:

"As you do these things you will gain more credibility. People may ask you to get the donuts and coffee a few times, but until you deliver the donuts and coffee on time, you are not competent at doing so, and do not, therefore, have credibility. Only after you have completed this task successfully can you claim competency and, therefore, be considered credible."

Remember people buy *you* first, *and then* they buy your ideas. What you lack in experience, you can make up in thoughtful communication of your unique insight. Before you communicate your unique insight, be sure to observe the company culture and political nature of the organization.

1. Show respect to those that do have the experience.

2. Learn what is expected of you. You have to know the territory you are in.

3. Remember to be observant.

4. When you *are* assigned to a project...go for it. Show them you can run with your ideas.

Once you have competence and credibility, you are more likely to be well liked and respected at work. Your hard work will win you the respect of your peers and managers. Best of all, your ideas will get the attention they deserve.

Body Language

How you say something at work is going to make more of a lasting impression and have a greater impact on your intended audience than *what* it is you actually say. If you want people to listen to you and take your ideas seriously (and we assume you do if you are reading this book), then it is important to consider how you are coming across to those you're speaking to. As Jan D'Arcy explains, people often focus more on your body language than they do your words.

> "Almost half the information we receive in a face-to-face meeting is from body language, eye contact, and facial expressions. The tone, volume, rate, and quality of the voice convey 30% of the information and the content or words contribute another 25%. Your body language, vocal expression, and message must be in harmony with each other for you to communicate effectively. If there is any discrepancy, your listeners will usually respond to your body language and voice, and question your words."

Picture yourself at a social event. You start to converse with someone. You're having a pleasant conversation, but after a few minutes you notice their eyes are starting to glaze over. Soon this person is looking all over the room except for where you're standing. What kind of message does this send to you? What impression have you formed about this person in your mind?

Make sure your body language is conveying the message you intend to get across. Merely saying the right things isn't enough to convince a person of your sincerity.

If you are distracted by something in the room, say so. It is much better to be genuine, especially if you're meeting someone for the first time.

While at a networking luncheon during a two-day event for women business owners in Chicago, Lisa, a young marketing professional, struck up a conversation with the woman sitting next to her at the table. As they talked Lisa started noticing the woman was glancing around at everyone at the table—except her. As other women at the table began to exchange business cards, the woman pulled out her purse and started handing out her own cards. She collected several from the other ladies and tucked them neatly into her purse. Afterwards she turned to Lisa and made a comment indicating she had been listening to their conversation. Lisa was shocked. The woman's body language conveyed she hadn't heard a word Lisa had said, and Lisa had already lost interest in continuing the conversation.

Make sure your body language conveys the message you intend to send to your audience. People pick up on these silent signals and form an impression of you. If you are meeting someone for the first time, you will not have another chance to make a good first impression.

Also important is your tone of voice. The tone conveys a powerful message to your audience. Your tone is separate from the words you use. Picture a candy bar that you buy at the grocery store. This candy bar is your message to an audience. If the candy bar represents your words, then the wrapper is your tone. Is your wrapper attractive or one that turns shoppers away?

Vocabulary

Your word choice says a lot about you. People with bigger vocabularies are generally considered to be more intelligent.

Studies have indicated that a person with a large vocabulary is promoted faster and higher than someone with a less than impressive repertoire of words. If you want to be successful, start learning some new words. Make it a goal to learn at least one new word a week.

You must also use your vocabulary tactfully. Consider the savvy caterer who has been asked to give a talk about how to throw the perfect dinner party. While speaking to an audience of young homemakers from the Midwest, the caterer may refer to a certain popular hors d'oeuvre as a "veggie tray." However, when speaking to a group of investment bankers in New York City, the same caterer may refer to the veggie tray as "crudités."

Why the two different words? It's about making a connection with the audience. If the caterer told a group of young homemakers from the Midwest to serve crudités at their party they may have thought him to be uppity or pompous. In New York City—where the term is more widely used—the investment bankers may have thought the caterer was an amateur if he'd said "veggie tray." This may be subtle, but it can be the difference between making a connection or not.

Connect With Your Audience

Making a connection is crucial if you want to be heard. You need to relate the information in a way that is palatable to the audience. This is where using vocabulary that is familiar to the audience will come in handy. Using the words people are used to hearing tells them you're one of them.

You need to get at who they are and understand what they want to know. Then tailor your message in a way that addresses the needs of your audience. If you want to watch a master at work, watch President Bill Clinton as he delivers a speech. He is superb at connecting with an audience.

Just remember: whenever you're talking to one person, or several people, first seek to understand where they're coming from and then tailor your message for them.

Know Your Audience

Of course, to connect with your audience you must have a good understanding of who your audience is. An effective communicator considers the audience before uttering one word.

In your early career you are most likely to be concerned with getting managers and peers to listen to you. At some point you may need to win over an entire auditorium full of people, but for now we'll concentrate on how to get your boss and coworkers to listen to you.

A few key questions to ask yourself before speaking are:

★ Is this the appropriate person to be talking to about this?

★ Does this person have the authority to move my idea forward?

★ Can this person deny my request?

★ What's in it for them?

Knowing your audience allows you to anticipate possible reactions to whatever you say. How are the people you are talking to likely to interpret what you have to say? What questions might they have? What do they need to hear to green light your initiative? Anticipating possible reactions gives you an opportunity to prepare appropriate responses ahead of time to questions or concerns. If you can predict someone's concerns, you can tailor your message to allay those concerns.

It's also important to know your audience so that you deliver the right message.

Anne once attended a speaking event at a university where the audience consisted mostly of executive women who were well established in their careers. The speaker was also a successful woman, however, she was unable to connect with the audience. Why? She addressed the roomful of executives as if they were college graduates just starting out in their careers. The speaker gave a very insightful and helpful presentation, but to the wrong audience.

Timing is Everything

When you say something at work makes a big difference. You want to approach people with your message at the right time, that is, when they are most likely to be receptive to listening to what it is you have to say. The minute someone walks into the office is probably not the best time to talk to them. Neither is the last five minutes before everyone is getting ready to leave.

You especially do not want to blindside anyone with a major request. Consider the following scenario.

Darla had spent two months working as an assistant for XYZ Company while she completed her degree. As graduation approached she decided to apply for a higher-level position. Darla asked her manager, Pam, if this would be a possibility. Happy with Darla's performance so far, Pam said she didn't see why not, and advised Darla to speak to HR. Excited, Darla typed up her resumé that night and marched right into the Director of Human Resources' office the next morning.

"Hi Tom. I'd like to talk to you about a full-time position. Here's my resumé. When do you have time to talk to me?" Darla handed Tom her resumé.

Taken off guard, Tom said he'd look it over, then he politely shooed Darla out of his office so he could get ready for a staff meeting. Looking back over her shoulder, Darla saw him put the resumé in a drawer before gathering his things and walking off to his meeting. She never heard from him and did not work for that company after she graduated.

What would you have done differently in this circumstance? What should Darla have done? First, she should have made an appointment with Tom. Second, she should have specified what type of full-time position she wanted to apply for. Let's revisit this scenario again.

After Pam advised Darla to speak with Tom in human resources, Darla spent a night typing up her resumé and cover letter. She researched openings at the company and spent a few hours considering how her own unique insights and life experiences would translate into transferable skills. The next day she sent a thoughtful and well-written e-mail to Tom.

Dear Tom,

I have been working as Pam's assistant for the past two months as I have been finishing my degree in nuclear physics. I have really enjoyed working here so far and would like to continue doing so after I graduate. I recently learned of the opening for a policy analyst and am submitting my resumé and cover letter for your consideration. Pam and I have discussed this, and it was she who advised me to speak with you.

At your convenience, I would appreciate the opportunity to speak with you in person to learn more about the opportunities that might be available to me. I am deeply interested in XYZ Company, and in pursuing a career here with the nuclear policy division.

Thank you. Please feel free to contact me at any time.

Best regards,

Darla

People who persuade others successfully come across positively, and understand how and when to convey their ideas to the right people.

Good Listening Skills

Of course, a hefty part of good communication is even better listening skills. Since you intend for others to listen to you, you must first demonstrate your willingness to listen to other points of view. Before you start nodding your head, yes, yes, you've heard this before; take a few minutes to consider whether or not you are a good listener. If you believe you are, try to write down a few thoughts about what makes you a good listener.

It is not enough to simply listen, or to be a passive listener. You must also learn how to be an active listener—someone who is fully engaged in the act of listening. How do you know if you are an active listener? People are considered active listeners if they tend to exhibit the characteristics below. Compare your notes.

★ Look the speaker in the eye for at least 5–7 seconds before looking away.

★ Ask open ended questions such as "tell me more," or "and then what happened?"

★ Do not make judgments indicated by comments such as, "I agree." "Oh, that happened to me too and it was awful." Beware of jumping in too quickly with advice: "Here's what you should do."

★ Body language suggests they are actively engaged in the conversation (i.e. active listeners do not turn away from the speaker).

★ Uses prompts (mm-hmm, wow, uh-huh) to encourage the speaker to continue.

★ Do not interrupt the speaker unless it's to clarify major points of what is being said and get the speaker to confirm or explain.

Active listening is harder over the phone, because you can't use the speaker's body language as a cue, but it's just as important as in person.

To practice your listening skills, ask a friend, significant other, or trusted colleague to do this exercise with you. Have your partner tell you something about themselves that you don't already know. Ask them about an ambition they have, a favorite childhood memory, an embarrassing moment—anything they are wiling to share. Just make sure they talk for at least 3–5 minutes, and as they speak, practice being an active listener.

Afterwards, repeat the main points back to them, and then request comments about your performance as an active listener. Did your partner perceive you as an active listener, or did you appear bored? Perhaps you came off as trying too hard. Take some time to evaluate the response you receive, and remember that every encounter with another person is an opportunity to practice your active listening skills.

When you are new to a company, it may take some time before people are willing to listen to you. You have to prove to be credible and to be competent. Don't get impatient. If you do a good job your managers will give you some room to shine. Use this time—when you don't have too much responsibility—to your benefit. Observe the political landscape of your company. How are decisions made? Who has the power to decide what initiatives are approved? Who are the members of the "in-crowd"? (i.e. Who is the boss most likely to listen to?).

Knowing this will be helpful later when you need approval for one of your own ideas or when you are up for a promotion. If you have observed the political landscape carefully you will know who the "right" people are to go to. If you don't think you need to pay attention to office politics then you must realize that you will probably have a very short career. Knowing how to maneuver within any type of organization is critical to your success.

In the next chapter you'll learn more about the secrets to a successful career.

Chapter Summary

★ You must have competence and credibility.

★ People have to buy you before they'll buy what you say.

★ How you say something has more of an impact on your intended listener than the actual message itself.

★ Know who your audience is and try to understand where they're coming from. You'll have a better chance of getting them to listen if you can make a connection with them.

★ Timing is key.

★ Your ideas are more likely to be heard if you are well liked and respected in your workplace.

★ Get buy-in from colleagues and managers who can move your vision forward.

★ When you present an idea, be sure to point out how others can contribute to its success. In other words, don't be a glory hound. Focus on the success of your projects, not on how much credit you'll get.

★ Do not blindside anyone with your idea.

★ Think before you speak.

★ Anticipate the reasons people may be resistant to your idea and come up with solutions ahead of time.

★ Be an active listener.

★ Be aware of the political landscape.

12 SECRETS TO SUCCESS

*"All our dreams can come true—
if we have the courage to pursue them."*

Walt Disney

We learned these secrets the hard way during our combined twenty plus years in the workforce. You're going to learn them in the next twenty minutes. It doesn't matter if your company is big or small, public or private, corporate or non-profit: you will give yourself an edge over other graduates by learning these secrets now. It's also important to understand the difference between knowing something and doing it, and to realize that it's the doing that counts.

At first glance, the secrets may seem like common sense. That's because for the most part, they are. The trick is to be able to do all twelve at the same time, every day. To really set yourself apart from your peers, look for ways to incorporate the action steps we've included in this chapter into your daily routine.

Secret #1:
Work Hard

Vince Lombardi, one of the greatest football coaches of all time, said:

"Dictionary is the only place that success comes before work. Hard work is the price we must pay for success. I think you can accomplish anything if you're willing to pay the price."

You must work hard if you hope to be successful. It's that simple. Work hard and don't expect everyone to praise you all day long either. You'll get a lot more accomplished and earn more respect if you care more about getting the job done and less about who gets the credit.

Action Steps:

★ Although we do not advocate working 24 hours a day, when you are just starting out you need to be perceived as someone who cares about and gives back to the company. Don't turn down assignments that require you to work overtime. On the other hand, don't take on more than you can reasonably handle.

★ Once you are seen as lazy it is very difficult to change people's perceptions of you. It is much better to start your career on overdrive than by coasting along in neutral.

★ Push yourself as hard as you can in the beginning of your career. Get as much experience as possible and never turn down an opportunity to learn from people more experienced than you. Even if you're staying late to make copies for an executive, use that time to ask them questions about how they got to where they are.

★ When you've pushed yourself as far as you think you can go, push harder. You will amaze yourself at how much better you can do.

★ Just getting by is not the same as getting ahead. Each time you complete a task, ask yourself if that was truly the best you could do. If your answer is no, do it again.

Secret #2:
Always Be Prepared

We can't stress this enough. "Always be prepared" means—seriously—always be prepared! If you have a presentation, know your material backwards and forwards.

Do not wing a presentation. It won't go as smoothly as you think. Anticipate questions you may be asked and prepare answers ahead of time. Don't assume your technology will work, either. Arrive early and test the equipment so that adjustments can be made. Have a back-up plan in case the equipment fails completely.

If you have a conference call scheduled, know who you will be talking to and exactly what the agenda is. Have any teleconferencing software set up and a conference room booked if needed. Several hours before the call, confirm that neither the conference line nor the meeting room has been double booked.

If you have an offsite client meeting, get directions in advance and know where to park. Your boss may decide to drive with you.

If a project starts to go awry, make the appropriate people aware of the situation immediately. Don't get accused of not raising the flag soon enough.

No matter what the situation is, be prepared for anything to happen.

Action Steps:

★ At the end of each workday, write down your list of to-dos for the morning. This is especially helpful to do on a Friday so you don't forget anything over the weekend.

★ When attending any type of recurring meeting, bring the notes or minutes from the last meeting. You'll be surprised how often this makes you look like a hero.

★ Anticipate possible problems and come up with solutions ahead of time.

Secret #3:
If You Want To Get Ahead, Lead The Way

You don't need to wait for someone to put you in a leadership position; you can show your company that you're a leader immediately. All you have to do is act like one. Create your own opportunities to flex your leadership skills. Take the initiative and offer to take on assignments or head up projects that others refuse to touch. Show your managers and peers that you aren't afraid of responsibility, and don't shirk accountability. Dare to be the go-to person; the person everyone knows will get the job done.

Action Steps:

★ Volunteer to be on, or chair, a committee.

★ Organize the company holiday party.

★ Head up a community outreach program to generate goodwill toward your company.

★ Offer to prepare the presentation no one else wants to do.

★ Don't be afraid to take risks.

Secret #4:
Dress for Success

People are going make a judgment about you and your abilities based on their first impression of you. According to the image experts, all you have is three-seconds to make a great first impression. If you do not win over your audience in those first three-seconds, you start at a disadvantage.

One of the worst ways to make a bad first impression is to dress inappropriately. There is no excuse for not researching the company culture and dressing accordingly. If you work for a software development company in California, jeans and tee shirts may be appropriate. However, if you are an investment banker you will need to wear nice suits.

People are going to assume you're as sharp as you dress so don't skimp on professional attire. When you are just starting out in your career you will set yourself apart from your peers by looking well put together. You will also feel more confident if you look professional, which in turn will make you act more confident.

People also judge your managers and your company based on how you look. Showing up to meetings looking scruffy, unshaven, or disheveled speaks volumes. If you feel as though you've been catching a little attitude from your boss lately, but haven't been able to pinpoint why, take a look in the mirror. You might not be making a good impression. Not only does this reflect poorly on yourself, but on your company as well.

Remember that "acceptable" does not have the same definition as "appropriate." "But no one says anything to me about the way I dress, so why should I care?" If you are asking yourself this question, then perhaps you should think about why you don't care to make a good impression. Don't you care enough about your job to dress appropriately? Your personal presentation says a lot about you and your level of self-respect. Think about what your image conveys and if that is the message you want to send.

You don't want to be overdressed either. Though it's better to be overdressed than underdressed, you can send the wrong message if you overdo it. This happened to Anne several years ago when she was working as the Director of Member Communications for the Committee of 200, a prestigious women's membership organization.

Each year C200 holds their annual meeting at a different location. In the summer of 2002, they decided to go to the Pierre Hotel in New York City to visit Ground Zero and to offer support to their colleagues working in the city. Before the conference, Anne went shopping for some new appropriate work clothes—the Pierre Hotel is quite upscale, plus they were going to pay their respects at Ground Zero. During a quick trip to her parent's house outside Detroit, Anne found several St. John suits on sale at a department store that was going out of business. Anything by St. John can cost several thousands of dollars, and she was able to buy a suit for only a few hundred. At the conference as she was making her way to the registration desk through a room where several women from C200 were seated, she heard one of them say, "Did you see that girl's St. John suit? We're obviously paying the staff way too much!"

Most of the time, however, dressing well is rewarded. Soon after landing a job on Wall Street, Joel decided he needed a nice suit. Not just a nice suit, but a *nice* suit. He spent about $1600. Not too long after, his boss chose three

"If you want to project a professional image in the workplace, realize this must be addressed on both the inside and outside.

To address the inside, the dialogue you have with yourself must be done in a more positive way. If you are always judging yourself, you will appear uncomfortable.

As for the outside, you must pay attention to manners and dress. Get some help, read magazines, walk through the department stores. At Nordstrom they have free consultants. Make an investment in quality. Tailoring is the key—your clothes have to fit well. They have to move with you and your body."

Jan D'Arcy
Executive Speech Coach
Author of *Technically Speaking* (Battelle Press, 1998)

employees to take to a business lunch. Not three entry-level employees, just three employees. Guess who was invited? That lunch put Joel on the boss's radar, and he made a great impression.

How other people dress at your level may not be the appropriate dress code. Look above you, not next to you, for fashion tips. We have always found "dress for the position above you" to be good advice.

Action Steps for Women:

★ Learn about fashion. There are wonderful resources online, on television, and in books and magazines.

★ Two simple things you can do are keep your nails manicured and your hair neat. It doesn't matter if you choose to have long or short hair, as long as you keep it well groomed. A good rule of thumb is to get your hair done about every six to eight weeks, and get a manicure about every one to two weeks.

Action Steps for Men:

★ Learn about fashion. There are wonderful resources online, on television, and in books and magazines.

★ Make sure your shirts are ironed and tucked in. If you wear a suit and tie, button your shirt all the way to the top. Yes, all the way. As a good friend of ours says, "A tie with an unbuttoned collar does not make you look relaxed, it makes you look drunk." If you can't stand to button the shirt all the way to the top, lose the tie. Your belt should match your shoes. Remember to shine them.

Secret #5:
Act with Integrity

People who consciously act with integrity are hard to fault because they go out of their way to do the right thing. They do not talk about coworkers behind their backs or speak negatively about an employer to a client.

People who act with integrity give every project their best effort and are very likely to be successful in everything they do.

Action Steps:

★ What does integrity mean to you? Try to think about this for at least once every few weeks.

★ Promote integrity in the workplace by complimenting others for acts of integrity.

★ If you have to respond to a customer complaint, do so without pointing out it was your coworker's fault.

Secret #6:
Have a Positive Attitude

Much of your success will be determined by your attitude and how you react to situations. Studies have shown that people with a more positive outlook live longer than their more negative counterparts. People like to hear positive messages at work. Employees with a "can-do" attitude are more popular because they inspire those around them. No one likes to believe the work they are doing is pointless or has no purpose. People want to believe in what they're doing. That's why it is so important to try to put a positive spin on any situation.

You have the freedom to choose your own attitude. Right now you can start projecting more positive energy out into the world. With just your attitude, you have the power to lift people's spirits, as well as your own.

Viktor Frankl was an Austrian neurologist, psychiatrist and a Holocaust survivor. In his book *Man's Search For Meaning* (Beacon Press, 2006) he reflected on his experience in the concentration camp, and wrote about the ability to choose one's own attitude.

"We who lived in concentration camps can remember the men who walked through the huts comforting others, giving away their last piece of bread. They may have been few in number, but they offer sufficient proof that everything can be taken from a man but one thing: the last of the human freedoms—to choose one's attitude in any given set of circumstances; to choose one's own way."

An important sentiment to remember always, not just at work.

Each morning take a few deep breaths to center yourself. Then go meet the world with a positive attitude. If something happens to dampen your spirits, take a few more deep breaths and look at the situation with a renewed sense of optimism. Remember that you choose your attitude and you have the ability to control your reactions to all situations.

Action Steps:

★ Always look for a way to be a part of the solution, not the problem.

★ If you have to deliver bad news, try to find a positive note to end on.

★ Do not be quick to assume the worst about a situation or person.

★ Surround yourself with people who energize and inspire you.

★ Remember that every situation at work is just a small "blip" on the big radar screen of your life.

Secret #7:
Treat Others with Respect

Regardless of their position in the company, treat everyone with respect. Though a certain structural hierarchy may exist within your company that gives you power over certain people, or vice versa, remember that people within that hierarchy are human beings. You'll get better results by treating others as people rather than titles.

Since you never know when a coworker will be on the opposite side of the hiring table, treat everyone as you would like to be treated, and you will be regarded favorably in the future. You also create a more pleasant work environment this way.

Action Steps:

★ Assume that everyone you work with has good intentions and is doing the best they can.

★ Give people the benefit of the doubt when they make a mistake.

★ Give credit where it's due.

★ Say hello to people that you pass in the common areas, even if you don't know who they are.

Secret #8:
Be Flexible

In *The Seven Spiritual Laws of Success* (Amber-Allen, 1993), Deepak Chopra says:

"You don't want to stand rigid like a tall oak tree that cracks and collapses in the storm. Instead, you want to be flexible, like a reed that bends with the storm and survives."

At some point in your career you are going to need to know how to survive a storm at work. If you work in an especially high stress work environment, you might face a storm every day.

People who cannot adjust to change are perceived as rigid. Not only does this cause them stress, but they're rarely promoted as well. Flexibility is key to surviving the storm and having a long, successful career.

Action Steps:

★ If you are assigned tasks that fall outside your area of responsibility, do not dwell on the unfairness of the situation. Consider this an opportunity to learn new skills that may come in handy later. Management will applaud you for your attitude, though they may not do so directly.

★ If your job description changes due to new management, a merger, or an acquisition, do not try to hold on to the old situation. Adopt the new, and prove that you can be counted on to be a team player.

★ Remember that to objectively assess any situation, you must not be married to one particular outcome.

Secret #9:
Learn How to Manage Your Energy

Stay sane during the initial years of transition between college and work by taking care of your body and being mindful of what you put into it. Taking care of your physical self helps keep your energy levels up during the workday and afterward—so you can go out with friends, spend time with your significant other, and pursue your hobbies.

If you keep your body fit, your mind will be able to handle so much more at work and in your personal life. It is so clichéd to say, "I just don't have enough time." Make time. Remember how alive you felt as a kid after playing outside all day during the summer? Your muscles might have been sore, but you felt as though you could conquer the world. When you stay fit as an adult, you can conquer the business world.

Jack Groppel, Ph.D., is a pioneer in the science of human performance and an expert in fitness and nutrition. His book *The Corporate Athlete* (John Wiley & Sons, 2000) teaches people how to maximize their performance at work, and in life, through proper diet and exercise. By reading his book you'll learn that energy is managed through our habits, not by willpower or self-discipline. According to Dr. Groppel, it takes twenty-one days to break habits, and ninety days to change behaviors.

You need to make it a habit to get enough sleep. Make it a habit to get plenty of exercise and eat the right foods. Only when you feel your best can you give your full attention to the task at hand. If you stay out drinking the night before a big presentation, you are not giving your best effort to that presentation. If you do not get enough sleep, you cannot expect to be fully engaged during afternoon meetings. While you may be physically present at work, you may not be mentally engaged.

Reading *The Corporate Athlete* at the beginning of your career is one of the best things you can do to get ahead. Not only will you learn how to manage your energy, but you'll also learn how to break the habits holding you back.

Action Steps:

★ Make it a priority to exercise a minimum of 30 minutes a day. Hire a personal trainer, join a gym, or just exercise on your own.

★ Create new habits that align with your desired lifestyle.

★ Read books about healthy eating and cooking.

★ Be disciplined to plan your lunchtime meals, or make good decisions when you go out for lunch.

★ Don't feel pressured to eat everything people bring into the office.

★ Don't be pressured into going out if you need rest.

★ Don't spend time with people that mentally drain you.

★ Use *all* your vacation time. Some companies don't allow you to roll over vacation year to year. It must be taken between January and December of the calendar year. A refreshed employee is a good employee.

★ Be as good to yourself as you are to your best friends.

Secret #10:
Keep Your Finances in Check

Financial stress can impact your work performance as well as your personal life. Don't begin the cycle of living paycheck to paycheck. Promise yourself you won't be a statistic. Don't do what the majority of people in the United States do by living above your means just to keep up with the Joneses.

The key is to know how much money you have coming in and how much you have going out. The easiest way to do this is to put it all down on paper, or put it into a spreadsheet. The most important step you can take on the road to financial freedom is to do a budget and live by it.

To create a budget, record everything you spend money on each month and add it all up. This might include: food, rent, clothing, entertainment, car insurance, utility bills, dry cleaning, cell phone, credit card payments, and school loan payments. Don't forget haircuts, coffee and all the little things that add up. Then compare it to your take-home pay. Cut your spending until you can save some money each month.

As a fresh college graduate you may have a tremendous amount of debt from school loans. If you don't you are extremely fortunate. Stay in good standing by paying them down on time or earlier, and you'll have excellent credit by the time you're ready to buy a house.

In addition, there are several don'ts:

- Don't get yourself into credit card trouble when you first get out of school. Move home if you have to, and start out slowly.

- Don't feel the need to furnish your first apartment with brand spanking new furniture. Look for used furniture, or items friends and family are planning to donate.

- Don't buy anything you can't afford to pay cash for.

It feels different—better—when you own things outright.

Action Steps:

★ Pay yourself first; take advantage of 401K programs at work and open a Roth IRA if you can.

★ Learn about investing. Watch Jim Cramer on CNBC's "Mad Money."

★ Set short and long-term money management goals the same way you do for your job search.

★ Check out "The Dave Ramsey Show." He is a personal finance expert and his radio program focuses on life, love, and relationships, and how they happen to revolve around money. It is available on local radio stations or online at www.daveramsey.com.

Secret #11:
Remember, You Are in the Driver's Seat

This can be hard to remember sometimes, especially if you're working for a company heavily steeped in politics or for a boss who repeatedly takes credit for your ideas.

Ultimately you are the driver of your own career and success.

It is up to you to make the appropriate people aware of what your interests are and what you want to do. You also have to find a way to make them care.

You are responsible for making management aware of your desire for a promotion and of your abilities. You need to prove that you are ready to handle the additional responsibilities.

Sometimes people are "promoted" into jobs they don't enjoy because their managers are in need of their particular skill set. If this happens to you, it's okay to speak up and ask what moving into this new position will mean to your career. Consider Joe's story:

After working three summers in sales, Joe knew what he wanted to do professionally after college. His people skills were off the chart; he was charismatic, good-natured, and honest. He was excellent at listening to his customer's needs, and he had established credibility among his customers and peers.

After school, Joe accepted a sales position at an international pharmaceutical company. He was excellent at his craft and received national awards for his sales efforts. But each time his managers offered him a promotion, he turned it down. Joe knew that his passion was not to be a manager, but to be in the field selling his products. Many of his colleagues questioned his judgment, and wondered why he chose not to climb the ranks of management.

Looking back, Joe is grateful that he had the self-confidence and self-awareness to pursue his career in sales. He is also grateful that his company respected his decision because some companies will fire you if you refuse a promotion. Why? Companies sometimes feel that they have invested in you and they want you to rise through the ranks of the company so you can help train others. This is another reason to choose the company you work for carefully.

Fortunately things worked out for Joe. At the end of a thirty-year career, he consistently ranked in the top 10–20% every year. He enjoyed a job where he could leverage his strengths, and which enabled him to be at home every night with his family.

Everybody has a different career path that will be right for them. Like Joe you should to pursue a career that is aligned with your priorities. Also, don't expect your managers to know what's right for you. While you may not know exactly what the next step is in your career, you do have the power to accept or reject each opportunity as it presents itself.

Action Steps:

★ Develop a good working relationship with your boss and let him or her know about your career ambitions.

★ Set up a meeting with your boss every month so you can keep the dialogue going.

★ Find a mentor, someone who is experienced and respected in your field, and meet with them regularly. Don't wait for people to come to you. Be proactive and seek out someone that you admire and want to learn from. Your mentor doesn't need to work at the same company you do either.

★ Don't stop at just one mentor. Create your own advisory board of more experienced professionals who you trust and who will be honest with you.

Secret # 12:
Enjoy the Journey

If time travel was possible, and reasonably affordable, we agree there is one thing we would go back and do. We would have appreciated each job, assignment, and performance evaluation for what they truly were: learning experiences that would prove helpful to us later in our careers.

We point this out because some people are so eager to achieve a position of power that they try to race to the top without considering the important lessons they should be learning in their current positions. This is a big mistake many young professionals make. Without a strong foundation of technical skills, time management tools, and personal relation techniques—skills that are critical to absorb now—you will be unable to reach the level of corporate maturity necessary to be promoted. After a promotion you will be too busy with other responsibilities to be able to go back and pick up those skills.

There are always going to be aspects of your job that you do not like, or assignments that you would rather not do. Instead of dreading these unappealing tasks, try learning something from them. You may have to get creative, but if you look hard enough, we promise you will pick up a trick or two that will be useful to you in the future.

Don't plan your youth away. Strive to have some structure and goals, but don't feel pressured to be there right now. Enjoy where you are.

Action Steps:

★ Don't waste energy stressing out over something you cannot fix. Only expend energy on solutions to problems, not lamenting the problem itself.

★ Look for ways to celebrate every achievement, no matter how small.

★ Live every day to the fullest and have a purpose in mind when you wake up each morning.

Chapter Summary

★ You will not achieve success without hard work.

★ Always be prepared. It's the best offense for a successful career.

★ Don't wait to be asked to take a leadership role.

★ Always look well put together and dress appropriately.

★ Maintain your integrity always.

★ Have a positive attitude and you will be an inspiration to yourself and others.

★ Be respectful of others.

★ Practice flexibility, even when things don't go your way.

★ Managing your energy is equally as important as managing your time.

★ Knowing how to manage your personal finances is key to reducing stress and being a productive employee.

★ Keep in mind that you control your career. Make decisions that are right for you and take responsibility for the decisions you make.

★ Enjoy the ride.

8

NETWORK LIKE A PRO

*"How many cares one loses when one decides
not to be something but to be someone."*

Coco Chanel

You may think it's enough to do your job well. It isn't. Having a network of people with whom to collaborate and learn from is critical to the longevity of your career. In this chapter we'll discuss the importance of networking and how to do it effectively.

Networking is like the Internet: it's about being connected. The Internet—constantly buzzing with activity and information—is always there for you to plug into. Your own personal network operates the same way and it's there right now waiting for you to take advantage of it.

Why should you concern yourself with networking at this point in your career? Don't you have enough on your plate? Well, make room. A good network is vital to career success. Developing a good network is like taking out a career insurance policy. If you find yourself out of work unexpectedly or want to find a more challenging position, you will have people to turn to. According to statistics from the Federal Bureau of Labor, close to 70 percent of all jobs are found through personal contacts. Less than 2 percent of all jobs are attained through blindly sending out resumés. You can't afford not to network.

A good network is also going to be vital to your personal success because it serves as a constant source of inspiration and encouragement. Investing the time to develop a robust network early in your career will give you a huge advantage over your less socially motivated peers. Taking time to build your network is also just a fun way to kick off your career.

Who is in Your Network?

Right now, you already have your own network. Surprised? You shouldn't be. After all, you started building it years ago. Who do you know? Who do you call for advice? These are the people who make up your current network. You can reach out to them and connect or reconnect right away. They can be friends, family, teachers, business associates, or anyone else you know.

"The best advice I ever received: manage your own career; network as much as possible; let managers know what you want to do long-term; and ask them if they have any stretch assignments."

Marketing Director
Age: 30
Michigan State University

Make a list of all the people you know. Categorize them by your connection to them, for example: teammate, co-worker, roommate, neighbor, teacher, coach, boss, family friend, etc. This will help you think of all the people you know in an organized way. Any one of these contacts might know of the perfect job opportunity for you.

You also belong to several other people's networks. Consider who else would want you to be in their network. Who are you able to help?

Always look for ways to expand your network. Using networking events as a way to make new friends is a wonderful way to expand your network, especially if you've recently relocated to a new city, state, or country for your job. Even if you still live in the town you grew up in, reach out to people from other cities and cultures. Having friends all over the world will make you a more well-rounded person and provide you with opportunities to travel and learn about different parts of the world. Whenever you meet someone new, jot down a few notes about them on the back of their business card so you have something to refer to later.

Common Misconceptions About Networking

Many people think of "networking" as those uncomfortable events at which a group of strangers gather around a half-empty buffet table and make awkward attempts at small talk. And while yes, networking can be like this (we'll address formal events later in the chapter) it doesn't have to be. If approached with the right attitude, networking can be a way to form new friendships and have fun. It can also be a source of personal growth.

The point of networking is lost on some people. The idea is to make connections, not transactions. If you take a genuine interest in others and help people reach their goals, you'll be successful. Don't look at networking only as a "what's-in-it-for-me" proposition. Ask others how you can help them.

When you're just starting out in your career, you may feel like you don't have much to offer. *Au contraire!* You probably know all about the latest blogs and online technologies, for one thing. Share some of your favorite online resources for industry news with the folks you meet and want to help.

Sharing information about yourself and what you are interested in may also help you in ways you cannot predict. Melissa, a computer sales representative, once attended a networking event where she met Ray, a business owner with a deep appreciation for fine wines. He talked to her about his experiences working in France, and traveling Europe visiting the finest vineyards and wineries. He did not know that Melissa was in the process of writing a book for executives to learn proper wine etiquette. Melissa and Ray never worked directly together in the computer industry, but they have met several times over dinner to discuss ways that Melissa can market her book.

Be Authentic

Networking is not about pretending to be someone you're not. The only way to be successful at networking is to be transparent with your intentions and never misrepresent who you are. If you are attending a networking event simply because you're curious about the host organization, say so. You also don't want to pretend you are knowledgeable in fields that you know little about. Don't feel pressured to feign experience or interest in something just to fit in. There is nothing more appealing to a new acquaintance than sincerity.

Be polite, but don't be phony. There is a big difference between the two and most people have a sixth sense when it comes to figuring out who is on the up and up and who is not. In our experience, the most successful people are those who genuinely enjoy meeting others and use networking events to do so.

Make it FUN!

Rather than thinking about networking as something you have to do, consider it an opportunity to meet people that may not otherwise have crossed your path. What can you learn from these people? Remember, everyone you meet in this world has had a unique experience. Meeting as many different people as possible is a great way to learn about other viewpoints, share ideas, and even find new interests.

Janie, a successful marketing director for a national retailing giant, discovered her love of fly fishing during an offsite company team-building trip. Janie and her colleagues were deposited on a remote riverbank in Arkansas, where Jack, an experienced fly fisher, guided them through the fundamentals of fly fishing. Jack was so touched by Janie's genuine enthusiasm for the sport that he invited her on a trip with his group of "regulars." After the trip Janie bought her own fly fishing gear and plans to pursue this hobby in her spare time. She has even converted her fiancé into a fly fishing enthusiast, and they both enjoy learning about the sport from their new friend Jack.

Networking as a Mirror

Meeting new people can teach you a lot about yourself. People who we haven't known for a long time have unique insight into how we are perceived by the outside world. Getting feedback from these new acquaintances can be an invaluable source of information about how you come across to others.

People who have known you for years will cut you some slack when you are disorganized, tired, or even argumentative. New acquaintances won't. They will simply assume this is what you are like all the time. Watching how new people react to you can tell you how you're likely to come across to a new coworker, a client, or a potential employer. Each time you meet someone new, remember to practice making a good impression. Don't be shy! The more people you meet, the more you'll learn.

Anywhere, Any Time

Networking can be the conversation you have with a new workout buddy at the gym. You can network while you ride the bus to work in the morning. If you take a pottery class you can fire up a network there. Whether you realize it or not, you are already networking every day of your life. "With who?" you ask? What about that person you casually chatted with at the beach; or the individual that just prepared your deli sandwich?

It will behoove you to treat every person you meet with respect and interest. Who knows if the woman serving up

Sloppy Joes at the deli counter also owns six local restaurants? The software your company sells may be just what she's looking for to streamline the payroll in her six locations. Strike up a conversation and you could be the one to make the sale.

You will never be able to know a person simply by looking at them, so treat everyone as if they are the next Oprah Winfrey. You should do this because you like people, not because you want something. When you are genuine, your intentions shine through and people want to help you. Use every opportunity, every interaction, as a chance to connect with someone new. Keep in mind that who you are is more important that what you do.

Organized Networking Events

Corporations, professional organizations, and associations of all kinds host formal networking events. You will attend several of these events during your career so you should know how to use them to your advantage.

Make a Great First Impression

It is critical to come across as someone others want to know. To make a good first impression, keep the following tips in mind:

★ Smile and be approachable

★ Dress well

★ Use appropriate body language

★ Have a solid handshake

★ Use good manners

★ Be genuine

★ Don't do all the talking

★ Show an interest in others

★ Turn off your cell phone before the event

★ Know proper networking etiquette

For the remainder of this chapter, we will focus on that last bullet point, proper networking etiquette. This is critical at formal networking events.

Business Cards

Make sure your business cards are sparkling clean and not worn. Never hand someone a dirty or bent business card. You should think if your card as an extension of yourself. You wouldn't show up to the event in dirty or wrinkled clothes would you?

To prevent your cards from getting beat up, keep them in a case. If you have one with your Alma Mater on the cover use it. This is a great invitation for others who went to your school to strike up a conversation with you. Many universities sell or give away luggage tags and business card holders to alumni because they want you to continue making connections with fellow alums after you've left campus. Of course, they don't mind the free advertising either. Contact your alumni relations office to find out if you can have a business card holder sent to you. Some schools may charge a small fee.

If your company does not provide you with business cards you can easily have your own personal cards printed to hand out at networking events. There are several online services that charge only a small fee for 250–500 cards. If you take advantage of one of these services, do not put your company logo on the cards. Some companies have very strict rules about branding and you do not want to get into trouble for simply trying to go the extra mile.

When you accept a business card from someone make sure to look at it before you put it in your purse or wallet. You do this for two reasons. First, this will help you remember the person who gave you the card. Second, it is a sign of respect. It is rude to take someone's card and put it away before you look at it. If you think of a compliment to extend, or come up with a question to ask, that's even better. Remember, a business card is an extension of the person giving it to you.

Set a Goal

It is always a good idea to have at least one goal when attending an organized networking event. Examples of goals you might have are:

★ I will talk to at least five different people

★ I will introduce myself to anyone who is standing alone looking uncomfortable

★ I will collect ten business cards

★ I will tell at least four people about my company

★ I will learn about someone else's hobbies

★ I will make plans with someone for coffee next week

Set goals that are right for you and for the occasion. Not only does having a goal make it more likely that you will be productive at the event, but later you'll be able to decide if this particular event is one that you should attend again. If you met people that you want to network with in the future, then you know this is a good event to come back to.

Have Small Talk Topics at the Ready

While you might not enjoy small talk it is important when you attend organized networking events. Have a few topics at the ready that are interesting to you. Choose topics you are comfortable talking about, and do not focus your entire discussion on yourself or your profession.

Read the newspaper before attending a networking event and don't skip the business, finance, or international news sections. Read up on the latest trends in your particular industry. Know facts and trivia about your hometown, current city, and sports teams from both. You should have enough interesting and relevant topics to keep you chatting for at least a few hours.

Don't be a Conversation Crasher

Be respectful of others when joining a conversation already in progress. If two people are talking animatedly and seem very engrossed on their topic, do not barge in to announce your recent promotion. Wait until there is a natural lull in the conversation before introducing yourself. If the conversation is not likely to end anytime soon, move on and come back later.

On the other hand, be open to others that wish to join your conversation. If you are in the middle of speaking and you can tell someone is waiting to talk to you, acknowledge the person with a quick nod, but finish your story. You can be polite without changing course mid-sentence. If the person has arrived at a break in the conversation, welcome them by offering a quick summary of what your group has been discussing. For example, "We were just talking about the Saints game on Saturday."

You also don't want to monopolize someone's time, nor do you wish to have your time usurped by one individual. If you discover you have a lot to talk about with one particular person, make plans to meet for coffee and then continue circulating.

Don't Drink Too Much

While it may be tempting to have a glass of wine or a vodka tonic before mingling with a roomful of strangers, don't. You'll need your wits about you. If you feel you have to drink at an event, check with a friend ahead of time for their opinion on how many drinks it takes for your voice to get louder and the alcohol to be noticeable. Then be certain you drink less than that.

If you are attending a networking breakfast, lunch, or dinner, make sure to remember your table manners. If you need a refresher course try reading *Emily Holt's Encyclopedia of Etiquette: A Book of Manners for Everyday Use* (Cosimo, 2005).

Don't Carry Excess Baggage to the Event

At a networking event—in a roomful of people you are probably meeting for the first time—the last thing you need is to be weighed down by a large purse or briefcase. Make sure you can maneuver easily. Put your business cards in an easy-to-reach place and bring plenty. Plan out ahead of time where you will put the business cards you receive.

Remember to look at each person's card before you store it away. If you've offered to send them something, said you'd call, or discussed something of interest, you might make a note on the back of their card so you don't forget. You also want to remember to contact the correct person about the particular topic you spoke about. There is nothing more embarrassing than contacting someone when you think they are someone else. It is also very difficult—sometimes impossible—to recover from that particular networking faux pas.

In addition, do not talk about problems at home or at work. A networking event is not a free therapy session. People do not want to be weighed down with your problems—they have enough going on in their own lives. Keep the conversation topics light, positive, and upbeat.

Dos and Don'ts of Networking

Do	Don't
Be authentic	Be sloppy
Talk about your interests	Drink too much
Offer to help others if you can	Interrupt a conversation
Follow through on any promises you make	Talk about personal problems, politics, or religion

"I wish that I realized the value of my personal network of contacts. Always feed the network by helping others, anticipating their career needs and life passions. Then, be sure to stay in contact with your network, updating them from time to time on what you are up to."

Product Manager
Age: 47
Southern Connecticut State University

Maintain Your Network

A strong network is the single most effective career advancement tool you can have. Therefore, it is critical too that you maintain your network. If you take nothing else away from this book, remember to keep in touch with the people you have worked to develop relationships with. There are several ways to do this.

Much in the same way a celebrity stays relevant in the media, you need to stay visible to your contacts. Make sure your profile is updated regularly in the alumni database for your college or university. A common practice is to send an e-mail every so often to the different groups you belong to. This is most appropriate when you change jobs, or have an exciting announcement to make.

Segmenting your correspondence is important. For example, draft one version of your e-mail update for contacts you consider friends, another for members of the association to which you belong, another version for clients, and yet another for potential clients. This is customizing your message. Your list of contacts could include hundreds of people and since you can't write a personal note to each one, at least tailor your message to each group.

Another way to stay visible to your contacts is to pass along any relevant information that may be useful to them. For example, if you come across an article online or in a magazine that you know would interest them, send it to them. Include a note wishing them well. Keep in mind that a gesture like this loses its impact and sincerity when you ask for something in return. You can also join online social networking groups like LinkedIn. If you do, be sure to keep your profile updated.

> "Take advantage of any connections, however distant they are, you have in the field in which you would like to work. I obtained a very difficult to find paid research assistant position at a top university because I emailed all of the professors in my undergraduate psychology department explaining my goals and asking if they had colleagues at other universities who might be hiring. Then I emailed everyone that they suggested."
>
> Clinical Psychology Graduate Student
> Age: 30
> University of Notre Dame

Chapter Summary

★ Make a list of everyone currently in your network.

★ Be authentic when you meet new people and be up front about why you are networking. Are you looking for a job, in search of information, or trying to promote a product? Tell people so they can help.

★ Look for ways to assist those in your network.

★ Make networking fun.

★ Use networking events as a way to gain more self-awareness. Pay attention to how you're coming across to the people you meet.

★ Networking can take place anywhere at anytime.

★ When attending formal networking events, have a goal in mind so you can decide later if that was an event you'd want to go to again.

★ Practice your ability to participate in small talk and have several topics prepared ahead of time.

★ Do not interrupt a conversation to introduce yourself. Wait until there is a natural pause in the conversation.

★ Refrain from alcohol at professional networking events or at least don't drink too much.

★ Don't talk about personal problems, religion, or politics.

★ At events, don't carry too many items so you can easily exchange business cards and information.

★ Always look for ways to expand your network and be sure to maintain it throughout your career.

9

WORKING WITH
DIFFICULT PEOPLE:
HOW TO SURVIVE & THRIVE

"A successful person is one who can lay a firm foundation with the bricks that others throw at him or her."

David Brinkley

Difficult people are a part of life. Dealing with challenging personalities every day at work can be just plain miserable. If you learn how to handle unpleasant coworkers and bosses early in your career you are sure to go far.

Between the two of us, we have worked for over forty different bosses and alongside hundreds of coworkers. While the majority of people we've worked with have been insightful, honest, hardworking, and caring individuals from whom we've learned a lot, a few have been less than delightful. In honor of the more painful experiences, we have included this chapter about dealing with difficult people. We have chosen to focus on the ten most difficult personality types we have ever worked with. Of course, all names have been changed.

In addition, we are not psychologists or medical doctors, and we do not claim to be experts in human psychology. We simply wish to offer our observations about some difficult folks we've worked with and share the coping mechanisms we have found useful.

Difficult Coworkers

The No Follow-Through Guru

One of the most frustrating types of personalities at work is the No-Follow-Through-Guru. These are the people who should be working for the airlines. They promise to come through, but never deliver on time. If they promise to have a report finished by 5 p.m., you'll still be waiting for it the next day at 10 a.m.. Offering a No-Follow-Through-Guru assistance with the task at hand yields no results. Ask them if they want you to jump in and help and you're likely to hear them say, "Everything is under control; you'll have the report in just a few minutes." Of course, you'll meet your grandchildren before you ever get a copy of that report.

The best way to deal with a No-Follow-Through-Guru is to not let them dictate the timetable. If the deadline is in six days, tell them it's in two. Make sure their boss knows what you are expecting from them and by when. Don't count on them to come through, but don't act like you think they won't. Give them the benefit of the doubt, but don't wait until it's too late to raise a red flag or arrange for a back-up plan. Anticipate all the possible outcomes and take steps to make sure your assignments don't suffer because of someone else's inability to deliver what was promised.

The Tattle Tale

With a Tattle Tale lurking about, the boss knows if you've left three minutes early before you're even in the parking lot. A Tattle Tale believes no detail about your work is too insignificant to be passed on to the boss, and they revel in watching the clock for you.

Boss: Good morning Loose Lips how are you today?

TT: I'm fine, but I don't think Tim's doing too well. He's 20 minutes late already.

Boss: Hmm. Have Tim come see me when he gets in.

The best way to deal with a Tattle Tale is to not give them anything to talk about. In most cases the boss knows exactly what a Tattle Tale's game is and doesn't want them around either. Tattle Tales waste much of the boss's time. Do your best to ignore them and don't give them a reason to select you as a target for their office games.

Tim: You wanted to see me boss?

Boss: I want to know the reason you were 20 minutes late today Tim. This office starts at 8 a.m. and I expect everyone to be at their desk then. You didn't even call me to tell me you'd be late. I think we have a problem here.

Tim: Um, I was in a meeting with accounting that started at 7:30 a.m.

Boss: Hmm. Tell Loose Lips to come see me. He's wasting my time!

The Credit Hog

Another personality you're likely to meet in the office playpen is the Credit Hog. This person contributes nothing more to the team project than anyone else, but swoops in at the last minute and takes all the credit. To hear the Credit Hog tell it, the project would have been a sure disaster were it not for the Credit Hog's heroic efforts to save the day.

The best way to shut down a Credit Hog is to call them out right away. Never let the Credit Hog take all the credit in front of the boss. You don't want the boss to think the Credit Hog really did all the work or proposed the money idea. Since your silence is confirmation of anything the Credit Hog says you need to speak up immediately. Furthermore, you'll look like a schmuck if you go complain to the boss later.

So how do you speak up to shut down a Credit Hog without coming across as a Tattle Tale? After the Credit Hog is finished taking credit for all your hard work, praise the more deserving members of the team; the ones whose contributions actually did contribute to the success of the project.

Credit Hog: Boss, if it had not been for my superior accounting skills, the team never would have been able to meet the budget requirements specified in the RFP. I am delighted to inform you that we have won the contract, and the client said our ability to meet their cost structure was the primary reason we beat out the other four companies.

Boss: Seems like you really came through for the team. Good job!

You: Boss, I'd like to acknowledge the great work that Jules and Lionel put into this. They really came through by cutting down on our material costs, which is what enabled us to come in under the budget.

Lionel: Well, if you hadn't found the supplier we wouldn't have been able to submit a bid on the project at all. That supplier really gave us the edge.

Boss: Well, sounds like you all did a terrific job!

By acknowledging the efforts of the other team members, you take the spotlight off of the Credit Hog. Chances are your teammates will catch on to what you're doing and praise your work also.

The Power-Monger

As long as you don't let them get under your skin the Power-Mongers can be some of the most entertaining folks to work with because these are the people who believe you should be reporting to them. They'll go to great lengths to give you assignments they have no authority to give you. They'll insist you request their approval before you do the smallest of tasks, such as send an e-mail to a client. They may even call you on your way to the office and ask you to pick something up for the boss. But you'll later discover it was the Power Monger himself who needed the emergency pick up service. If you call them on their office hi-jinks it can be pretty amusing to watch them squirm, but if you let them walk all over you your workday can be a miserable experience.

There are two major categories of Power Mongers. There are those at the same level as you—though they may have been with the company longer—and those at a higher level than you, but to whom you do not directly report. Each type of Power Monger must be dealt with in the same way.

Your goal is to stop the Power Monger from wasting your time with assignments that do not fall within your scope of responsibility. If you concentrate on projects for which you are not ultimately responsible, it is a waste of company time and your boss will eventually come down hard on you, not the Power Monger. It is your job to discourage the Power Monger from interfering with your work.

Always try to deal with a Power Monger on your own first. You may be left with no choice but to go to the boss in the end, but always try to handle the situation yourself first. Most bosses are not impressed by a new hire that needs them to mediate a squabble between coworkers and that's basically what this situation boils down to.

So how do you turn this potentially career damaging situation into entertainment? Here are some examples of ways to tactfully discourage a Power Monger at the same level as you from mongering.

Power Monger: I saw the presentation you prepared for tomorrow's meeting. I think you need to redo it. Make it bluer.

You: Hmm. The boss approved it yesterday. I could tell him you have an issue with his decision, but considering how busy our schedule is for the next two weeks I'm not sure he would appreciate the interruption.

Don't be passive aggressive, but make it clear you will not be intimidated by the Power Monger, nor do you agree with his comments.

Power Monger: (calling you) The boss wants you to pick up coffee for her and I. Also, you need to buy a book of stamps on your way in.

You: Thanks Power Monger. Could you transfer me to the boss? I wanted to ask her a question before I got in and you just saved me a phone call.

Boss: Hi there, what can I do for you?

You: I just wanted to check with you about the best way to purchase items for the company. Power Monger informed me that you've requested stamps and coffee. Should I put this on my credit card, or pay cash and get reimbursed from petty cash? I'm unclear about the best way to do this to cut down on the paperwork for you.

Boss: I never told him to tell you to get those things. Just come into the office. I'll take care of Power Monger.

Of course, there is always the possibility that the boss did ask the Power Monger to ask you to pick a few things up. Survey the political landscape of the office before you say anything. If the Power Monger is the CEO's pet or a favorite of your boss, then you might be forced to put up with their shenanigans—however annoying they might be.

If the Power Monger is one or several levels above you be respectful during any interaction you have with them. If they attempt to task you for work that is clearly out of the realm of your responsibility, decline politely and be brief.

Power Monger: Oh! I'm so glad I ran into you. I need you to write up an estimate for me about the new project. I need it by Wednesday.

You: Hi Power Monger. I had really been hoping our team would get that project. I hear you're doing a great job with it. I'm actually leading another project at this point and I'm on my way to present it to the boss right now. Good luck with your project.

If a manager to whom you do not directly report continues to assign work that is clearly not your responsibility, inform your boss. Your boss will most likely halt the situation. However, don't be shocked if your boss directs you to do whatever the other manager asks. Your boss may not have much authority over this person, or they could be a favorite of the higher ups. Again, it is important to understand the political situation in the office so that you learn how to maneuver successfully within it.

The Suck-Up

There's at least one of these in every office. Instead of concentrating on getting their work done, they exert vast amounts of energy agreeing with everything the boss says. Nothing is out of bounds for the Suck-Up to trumpet as being the cleverest, most radically novel and brilliant idea ever conceived—as long as it was the boss's idea.

While the Suck-Up's ability to flatter even the most discerning of senior managers may advance them through the ranks, don't be tempted to pucker your own lips. Eventually the Suck-Up's luck will run out because their success is wholly dependent on the approval of the managers above them. Even a Suck-Up who wins the corner office will soon feel claustrophobic within it as the weight of his incompetence presses upon him.

The best way to deal with a Suck-Up is to do the best job you can and leave the Suck-Up to his own demise. As long as the Suck-Up doesn't start interfering with your work, simply ignore him.

When Your Boss is the Difficult Person

It is important to make the distinction between a bad boss and just a bad management style. You can learn a lot from a boss even if they can sometimes be difficult to deal with. Your boss may sometimes make decisions that you don't agree with. Before you assume they don't know what they're doing take a moment and realize your boss has different responsibilities and priorities than you do. You may not be aware of the larger picture.

On the other hand, if you find yourself working for someone that you cannot respect, due to unethical behavior or other actions that you cannot condone, then you may be justified going over your boss's head. However, you should be prepared to look for another job if you choose to do so.

This chapter assumes that your boss is a good person with a management style that is difficult for you to handle. Here are some examples of the most challenging managerial styles in the workplace. Now let's learn how to deal with some of the more difficult bosses you may find yourself working for.

The Micromanager

Even though micromanagers are probably the most often complained about type of bosses, it is often hard to define exactly why they are so annoying. This is because each act of a micromanager, by itself, may not be so bad. When the whole package is put together, though, these people become difficult to deal with.

What is a micromanager and how do you know if you are working for one? Here are a few behaviors often displayed by Micromanagers:

- Will not allow any decisions to be made without their approval.

- Requests your attendance at unnecessary meetings that waste your time.

- Forwards overwhelming numbers of "FYI" e-mails, which have no relation to any of your assignments. Then puts you on the spot during meetings by requesting updates relating to the subject matter of these e-mails.

- Insists on updates regarding your work so frequently that you are unable to do any work.

Here are some suggestions about the best way to deal with a micromanager in these specific situations.

Because a micromanager will not allow any decisions to be made without their approval, you need to be proactive and solicit their input without having to be asked for it. If they ask you to do a report and the report is due in one week, finish it early ask them to look it over and make comments two days before it's due. If they ask you to buy some new item for the office, do not purchase it until you have asked their opinion. They may act like they want you to do a task on your own, but they want to be involved in the decision making process.

If your boss sets up numerous meetings, which do nothing but waste your time, unfortunately there is not a whole lot you can do. You may be forced to sit through these unnecessary meetings. But block off time in your calendar for any assignments you're working on. This way when your boss tries to send you a meeting request, you will already show up as having something scheduled. Your boss may come and ask you to rearrange your schedule, or they may not. Your best defense against a micromanager is a good offense.

Create a separate e-mail folder just for messages from your boss to help manage online communications more effectively. Each time you receive a "FYI" e-mail, read through it to determine why they are sending it to you. Then write your boss back immediately and clarify what they expect you to do with it. For example, "Would you like me to follow-up on this? Please let me know how I can be of assistance?"

By acknowledging your receipt of the e-mail right away, you are being proactive and showing initiative. You are saying, "I have received the e-mail, what do you want me to do with it, and I'll keep you posted on the progress." If they don't really know what they want you to do with the e-mail, but want to throw it on someone else's plate to avoid their own manager accusing them of dropping the ball, you are saying, "Let me know when you decide what should be done with this."

You also have documentation, should it ever come to that, that you were on top of the situation. This way, you can keep track of exactly what they are asking you to do, and you are less likely to be caught off guard later. Review all e-mails at the end of each week, to keep them fresh in your mind. Anne used to keep a folder titled "LTBMITB" which stands for e-mails that are "Likely-To-Bite-Me-In-The-Butt" down the road. That way she could refer to them easily.

The best way to deal with constant requests for updates about your work is to Communicate, Communicate, Communicate! Having someone over your shoulder all the time can be less than motivating, but since you cannot change your boss's behavior, you'll need to focus on your own reactions. Try to make it a game and see how many times you can give your boss the information before they ask you for it.

The Workaholic

For their own reasons, these people work from dawn to dusk. What can you do if you work for someone that spends 24/7 at the office and expects you to do the same? Understand that workaholics frame their entire world through the lens of what they accomplish at work.

The best way to deal with a workaholic is to set boundaries early, and do not waver. If your scheduled hours are 9 a.m. to 5 p.m., never stay past 5:30 p.m. Politely refuse to say why you can't work all weekend. Turn off your pager when you aren't officially on call.

Workaholics also like to feel needed at the office. Ask their advice about projects and assignments that are challenging for you. Because they spend so much time working, they are a great resource of information. Try to take advantage of their years of experience.

The Magician

How do you solicit feedback about your job performance from a boss who is always performing a "vanishing act?" If your boss is never in the office, you may be struggling to determine exactly what is expected of you. Don't panic.

Simply make a list of the assignments and projects you are working on. Jot down what you are doing for each, and when you expect to be finished. Send an e-mail to your boss weekly. Ask if you need to prioritize anything differently. If you do not get anything back, just keep doing what you're doing.

You can also leave your boss weekly updates on voicemail. Keep these messages short and to the point. If you take the initiative instead of lamenting their absence, chances are your boss will see you as someone who can lead the team and get things done.

The Bully Boss

Some bosses are more like bullies than managers. They yell and scream and berate their staff just because they can. Learn how to push back appropriately and you will impress your Bully Boss. Push back the wrong way and you could get fired. If any of the following scenarios sound familiar, you may be working for a Bully Boss.

- Boss makes ludicrous accusations and then does not allow you to speak in order to defend yourself or explain the situation.

- Boss puts you down in front of coworkers or in client meetings.

- Boss makes outrageous requests and then questions your competence in private or in the presence of others.

You have to let a bully boss know that you won't tolerate their repugnant behavior; and you must draw the line they're not allowed to cross early in the working relationship. At some point you will have to confront your boss about their unprofessional behavior. Do not get emotional and do not raise your voice. If a Bully Boss tries to bait you by saying something personal, ignore the statement and stick to the issue at hand. Consider the following scenario.

It was only 1 p.m. when David finished preparing his boss's presentation for the board meeting later that evening. With four unexpected hours to spare, David realized this was the perfect opportunity to start researching the invoicing procedure that his boss wanted restructured. It was David's first year with the consulting firm and he was eager to get noticed.

David closed his office door behind him and walked down the steps to meet with the accounts payable staff. Two hours later, as David was talking with the supervisor of the department, his boss walked by and noticed David drinking a soda and chatting with Greg.

Bully Boss: David! I can't believe you're sitting here chitchatting when you have a board presentation to deliver to me by 5 p.m. today. Get up. Go to your desk and do the work we pay you for.

David: Actually I was just...

Bully Boss: Didn't you hear me? I don't know how I could have possibly made myself clearer. What part of your synapse is misfiring? Let's go, now.

David follows his boss back upstairs to their offices. As his boss entered his own office, David saw him notice the board presentation lying neatly on his desk. David was furious and decided to confront his boss right then. He reminded himself to stick to the facts of what had just happened.

David: I left you a voicemail a little before 1 p.m. to inform you the presentation was finished and to let you know that if you wanted to go over it together I would be in the accounts payable office researching the invoicing procedures that you asked me to look into. To complete the restructuring of the invoicing procedure, I am going to need Greg's help. I'm concerned that my credibility with him may have been damaged by your implication that I was wasting time in accounts payable when I should have been working on a presentation for you. He doesn't know that my work was completed because you did not give me the opportunity to respond to you down there. I can understand how you may have been concerned to see me somewhere other than in my office if you weren't aware the work was finished. However, if this is how you intend to handle these kinds of miscommunications in the future, I'm concerned about how we're going to work together.

The Bully Boss may get even more brutish at this point, or they may apologize. You cannot control their behavior, but you can control your own. Address the situation calmly and do not get emotional. Be polite and keep strictly to the facts. Keep in mind that you are attempting to resolve an issue, not win an argument. Your goal is make the Bully Boss realize that it is no fun to pick on you because you refuse to take the bait. You also stick up for yourself and refuse to be pushed around.

The Know-it-All

A Know-it-All is someone who always thinks their opinion is the most important and most accurate. They feel their ideas should be listened to, but have little patience when it comes to hearing what anyone else has to say. They have an opinion about everything and want to be in charge of every project. A Know-it-All does not want to be held accountable for anything that goes wrong, but does want the credit for everything that goes right. Fortunately, these types of coworkers are easy to spot. Unfortunately, they're difficult to work with.

When dealing with a Know-it-All, the first thing you have to remember is not to let this person get under your skin. They are going to act like this no matter what you do. You cannot change their behavior, so you must concentrate on achieving the best possible working relationship you can. Demonstrate that you are eager to listen to the Know-it-All, and even ask clarifying questions so they know you are taking them seriously: practice being an active listener.

Ask their opinion before they offer it. Remember, the goal is to get the work done without them holding up the process with rants about how much more they know than you.

For example, "Paul, I know you did it that way in the past and it seems to have worked well, so what do you think if we build on your idea and add XY and Z? Do you have some suggestions for how we move forward?"

In this chapter we discussed many different types of people you might come across in your professional life. While it is important to be aware of how others act, it's equally important to see yourself as your office mates do. If you are one of the difficult people described in the chapter, it might behoove you to evaluate your perception in the workplace.

In addition, remember that someone who exhibits bad office behaviors is not necessarily a bad employee or bad person. Everyone has a unique personality, and it's your responsibility to learn how to handle all different kinds if you want to be successful.

> "When addressing a difficult person's inappropriate behavior - no matter how difficult an employee has been - treat them with respect, dignity and compassion. Don't let your emotions, or theirs, influence your actions."
>
> Human Resource Executive
> Age: 54
> Ohio State University

Chapter Summary

Throughout your career you will encounter people that are challenging to work with. If you're able to identify and address the specific behaviors that are difficult to deal with, you'll stand a better chance of developing good working relationships with even the most annoying of office personalities.

Five of the most challenging coworkers you are likely to come across at the office:

- The No-Follow-Through-Guru
- The Tattle Tale
- The Credit Hog
- The Power-Monger
- The Suck-Up

Five of the most difficult bosses to work for:

- The Micromanager
- The Workaholic
- The Magician
- The Bully Boss
- The Know-it-All

10

TIME TO MOVE ON

*"Twenty years from now you will be more disappointed by
the things you didn't do than by the ones you did do.
So throw off the bowlines.
Sail away from the safe harbor.
Catch the trade winds in your sails.
Explore. Dream. Discover."*

Mark Twain

Eventually the time will come for you to move on from your first position. This chapter talks about how to transition when you decide to leave, and what do to if your employer decides for you.

There are six common scenarios that are likely to unfold when the time comes to move on from your current position. You may join a company you love only to realize later that you hate the job you were hired for. Conversely, you may love your job, but discover you hate the company. Or, you enjoy your job and your company, but dislike your industry. Additionally you could be laid off or fired. Finally—and one of the most fun ways to move on—you could be promoted. In the next few pages you'll learn some tips about how to approach each situation.

I Love My Company—I Hate My Job

What if, after a few months on the job, you still like the company you're working for, but you dislike your functional area? Let's say you're in sales, but would rather be in marketing. What should you do?

First, find out if marketing is hiring. Do not go directly to the marketing department to do this. Go to the company's web site, or check out the job postings in the break room—or elsewhere in the building. Even if there aren't any positions posted now, there may be a position opening soon.

Keep your eyes and ears open while you're in the office. Maybe someone is being promoted or getting ready to retire. Departments sometimes hire two new employees to take over the job duties of one long-term employee. Of course departments also sometimes phase out certain positions when an employee retires or moves on. The point is, don't make a move until the right opportunity comes along. Don't be impulsive when it comes to your career.

Make friends in the marketing department, but don't tell them you want to leave your current position. News like that travels fast in an office. Nobody needs to know what you're thinking until you're ready for them to—especially your boss. It's important to talk to your boss before anyone else—just be sure to pick the right time.

If the deadline for your department's biggest project is approaching, now is not the time to ask to move to a different area. Wait until the major projects are finished before you approach your boss. Then, choose a time when they will be most receptive to hearing you out. Don't approach them ten minutes before they have to leave for a meeting.

Pick a time when they are relaxed and can focus on your conversation.

Keep in mind that nobody likes to lose a good employee. So don't expect your boss to be elated when they hear you want to join another team. Your boss may even take it personally. Their ego could be bruised because you no longer want to work for them. To prevent hurt feelings—to the extent you can—be positive in how you approach the situation. Let your boss know that your decision to pursue another functional area has nothing to do with them.

> **You:** I really enjoy working for you in the sales department, and I like working at XYZ Company. In fact, in the past nine months I have become even more committed to having a long career here at XYZ. But I've realized that my true interests are in marketing. I was hoping you could talk me through what my options are here. I am coming to you first because I value your opinion, and wanted to talk to you about this before I do anything else.

> **Boss:** Well, I'm disappointed to hear you do not see a future in sales, but I appreciate you coming to me first. Let's see what we can do to keep you here at XYZ Company.

If your boss is amenable to you transferring to the marketing department and is willing to help you, set up an action plan to make the transition quickly. You don't want any resentment from your team members to make sticking around uncomfortable. You also don't want your boss to suddenly decide to try to keep you. If other people on your team suddenly decide they like marketing too, your boss could put a stop to any transfers to ensure there isn't a mass exodus from the sales team. Your goal is to make the move happen sooner rather than later.

What if your boss is willing to help you make the move over to marketing, but only if you agree to stay in sales for more time than you want to? In this case, you may need to be flexible and stay as long as they need you. After all, if they are helping you make the move into another department, you owe them.

On the other hand, you may also need to assess how honest your boss is being with you. Try to determine their motives for wanting to delay the move. Are they trying to get you to change your mind? Maybe they've learned there won't be room in the budget to replace you, and now they're less motivated to assist you. Perhaps your boss thinks the director of marketing is a pompous jerk and is just trying to protect you from joining an unhappy team. There could be a dozen reasons why your boss promised to help you, and then drags their feet.

What if your boss reacts badly to the news and makes it clear they do not support this idea? In this case, you might be in trouble. Your boss may not want you on their team anymore now that you no longer desire a career in sales. Your boss may attempt to have you fired so they can hire someone new that wants a career in sales. Your boss could transfer you to a division you are not interested in. Just be aware of the possible outcomes before you do anything you can't take back.

If you have a supportive Human Resources department or higher managers, you could try going to them if the meeting with your boss doesn't go well. Make your boss look as good as possible. Tell them that you feel you may have said something wrong to your boss when you were merely trying to explain your desire to switch departments. Explain to HR that you like the company and were just trying to find out if there was a possibility for you to move into the marketing department. They may be motivated to help if you are a good employee.

As long as you have informed your boss, you are now free to talk to people in other departments. Ask the folks in marketing what they do and how they like their individual job descriptions. Talk to others outside of your company to find out what different careers are possible in marketing.

If your company does offer you a chance to interview with another department prepare twice as carefully as you would for a normal job interview. Someone could be pulling some major strings for you: make them look good, and make yourself look good too. You might get a lateral move, or you may be offered a position down one or more levels from where you currently are. The company wants to see that you're willing to work your way up. If this is truly the path you want to take, go for it. Sometimes you have to take two steps backward to go five steps forward. And better to go for it earlier when you're used to student living.

I Love *Parts* of My Job

Perhaps you like your functional area, but dislike the particular industry. You work in public relations for a pharmaceutical company, but you would rather work in public relations for the hospitality industry. This means you're going to have to switch companies and start your job search all over. This time, however, you have experience in your chosen field. Now all you have to do is convince employers that your skills can be easily transferred from the pharmaceutical industry to the hospitality industry. This is much easier than getting your foot in the door when you have no experience at all. It is also much easier to find a job when you already have one.

As you start looking for a new job do not tell anyone at your current company that you're looking. A coworker might let it slip to the boss. If your company finds out anyway, and your boss asks you to confirm that you are looking for a job, you can be vague. Honesty is not the best policy in this situation.

> **Boss:** I hear you're looking for a new job. How's that going?

> **You:** I researched an opportunity that was brought to my attention just as I would any potential opportunity for career advancement. In the end it was nothing I wanted to consider.

Of course if you are still considering the offer, don't say that last part.

Don't use the company e-mail or fax to send resumés to potential employers. If e-mail is monitored at your company you could be leaving sooner than you planned. Hopefully you have spent at least a year with this company. Employers often look down on applicants that have a history of job jumping or staying with a firm for short periods of time, because it's expensive to hire and train a new employee. A potential employer will want to know you're committed to staying for several years before moving on.

When you receive an offer, get it in writing before submitting your notice to your company. You do not want to find out the offer has been rescinded or modified unfavorably after you quit your current position.

I Love My Job—I Hate My Company

If you enjoy your job and industry, but dislike your company it's time to search for another organization. You should try to stay at a company for at least one year though before moving on. Many employers are wary of job jumpers. You do not want to be labeled as such.

You may also need to consider how strict the noncompete agreement is that you signed when you started. If you didn't have to sign one, there's nothing to worry about, but increasingly companies are requiring these. Dust off your copy and look for any potential problems.

Though it may be difficult, try not to let on that you don't enjoy working at your company. Chances are if the

"Finding a company that fits you is as important as finding a job that fits you. I was lucky to find the perfect first job, but it was with the completely wrong company. It was like having a boyfriend that was tall, dark and handsome, but who couldn't carry on a conversation to save his life. It won't work no matter how hard you try so you just have to end the relationship."

Employment Coordinator
Age: 29
University of Central Florida

atmosphere is so bad that you are considering leaving, other people don't like working there either. This does not give you the green light to go around gossiping about upper management or complaining to coworkers about how unfairly you are treated. Keep your mouth shut, your eyes on your own work, and look for another job—but not on company time.

I Got Fired

Don't panic. It's not the end of the world. Unless you're embezzling money or doing something else illegal, footage of you being escorted out of the building is not going to run on the nightly newscast. If it's just a normal run-of-the-mill sacking, the best thing to do is to keep your wits about you.

There are several questions that you should try to get answered before you leave the premises. If you have signed a noncompete agreement when you were hired, confirm that you will no longer be expected to honor it. This is usually the case, but double check. Make sure you know who to contact for information about rolling over your 401K. You should have this information at home, but if you don't, make sure to ask for it.

If you have health insurance through your company, it will most likely be discontinued at the end of the month. Your company will send you paperwork in the mail within the next week, which explains how to sign up for Cobra, or interim healthcare coverage. Do not ignore this paperwork. You're only granted a certain window of time to sign up for this extended coverage. If you don't, you lose your health insurance completely.

You may be escorted out of the building without being allowed to retrieve any personal items from your desk. If this is the case, ask when you can expect to receive those—especially if you have anything important in your desk.

If you are fired for a particular cause, you probably previously received a verbal or written warning. The fact that you're being fired really shouldn't come as a shock. If it does, make sure to state that you weren't aware of any prior complaints regarding your work. You'll want to know what you could have done to prevent this from happening so that you can avoid a similar situation in the future.

Don't take it too hard. People get fired. It happens. Learn from your mistakes and move on. Getting fired can actually be a relief. After all, it's difficult to excel at a job you don't enjoy or if you're in over your head. Perhaps this is a sign that you're in the wrong field. This could be the best thing that ever happened to your career and now you're free to pursue something you'll truly enjoy. You have an opportunity to start over; so don't waste it. Do some self-reflection. Did you really want to be in that job?

While your manager may not want to give you a reference, some of your former colleagues might. Keep in touch with them via e-mail. When it's appropriate, ask if they would be willing to be a reference for you.

Even if you cannot count on this company for a reference, take comfort in the knowledge that they can't say much bad about you. They can confirm the dates you worked there and not much else. Think about if there's a coworker who thinks you were doing good things (and can speak about things you did do well—working with people, team leader from a project, etc.) and if they are willing to be a reference, but don't pressure people. If you were only there three months, you might not even want to put this company on your resumé.

If you decide to include this position on your resumé, be up front about why your employment with that company ended in job interviews. "I was let go because of X, and this is what I learned from it." Or, "It was a bad fit because Y." Show maturity and self-awareness.

Do not call your clients and badmouth the company (this should be obvious). This could get you into major trouble down the road.

Layoffs

Don't panic. Even in a good economy layoffs sometimes occur. Ask questions similar to the ones you would ask if you were fired. In addition, ask if there will be severance or assistance in securing a new job. Sometimes outplacement services will be offered, and if they are be sure to take advantage of them.

Go slowly when cleaning out your desk. Sit there for a few minutes and look around. Remember to take personal items and contact information for coworkers. If your rolodex is your own, don't leave it behind.

Don't leave without speaking to your boss. "I enjoyed working with you. I hope you found my work satisfactory." Ask if they'll be a reference for you in the future; most of the time they will.

Now it's time to contact people in your network that may be able to help you find another job. Try to stay positive and upbeat. You have an opportunity to find an even better job now.

I Got Promoted!

Don't panic. You're going to do great. First, take time to celebrate with family and friends. Do something fun to mark this milestone in your career. If a boss or mentor played a key role in helping get the promotion, now is the time to express your appreciation. A heartfelt handwritten note is appropriate and always appreciated. This is part of maintaining your network, as discussed in Chapter 8.

Negotiate salary and perks if appropriate (it probably is). Order new business cards that have your new title printed on them. Consider joining one or two professional organizations to expand your network if you haven't already. Subscribe to relevant trade publications and newsletters. Become a source of knowledge for others in your office. Make it clear that your managers were correct in selecting you for the promotion by working even harder.

Dressing for success is even more important now and you'll be expected to set an example. You'll probably be attending more meetings and be introduced to new people as a representative of your company. Adjust your dress and presentation to your new position. Don't brag about your promotion to your coworkers. Take it in your stride.

Chances are you have a new boss and you'll need to figure out how best to work for them. They may have a style that is different from what you're used to. Be observant to determine what styles they reward.

You can also get promoted into a position you're not ready for. If there are areas you feel incompetent at, find ways to learn. Enroll in accounting classes to help you tackle the new budget you're responsible for. Talk to mentors and others in your network. Don't bite off more than you can chew. Tell them up front if you're not sure about an assignment; seek out information rather than getting in over your head.

Sometimes the hardest thing to learn is delegation. Make sure you give clear instructions, and help your staff with their professional development. Don't be the micromanager or any of the other bad bosses.

What if everyone who has been promoted to this position before you has been fired? This is definitely something to be concerned about. Sit down with your new manager as soon as you are offered the position and ask what their expectations of you are. You may even want to inquire why you were selected. If the answer doesn't sound right, or you suspect you are being set up for failure, remember it's OK to turn a promotion down. Big companies will usually offer to promote you more than once before categorizing you as happy where you are.

Even in your fabulous new position, don't get so caught up in your job that you forget to have a life too. Enjoy your job, enjoy your life, and keep working hard until you achieve your definition of success.

Chapter Summary

★ Look for a way to transfer into a more rewarding role if you enjoy working for your company, but dislike your position. If possible, enlist the assistance of your boss. Make friends with the staff members in the department in which you wish to work. Be realistic about the timeline for a potential transfer and be patient.

★ If you like your job, but dislike your industry, you'll either have to get over it or look for another job. Make sure to keep a list of your transferable skills and accomplishments to present to interviewers if you decide to move on.

★ If you love your job, but dislike your company, try to hang in there for at least one year to avoid being labeled as a job hopper. Then, look for another job and make sure to take your time carefully researching the companies you're considering.

★ Don't panic if you get fired. Learn from your mistakes and move on gracefully.

★ Don't panic if you get laid off. You will most likely receive a good recommendation from your boss and you can start job-hunting by contacting members of your network.

★ The best way to move on is to get promoted. Remember to dress the part and take your new responsibilities seriously. Being promoted is a good indication that you are well on your way to a successful career. Prove your managers made a good decision by selecting you for the position. Work even harder.

CONCLUSION

Our vision for you is a successful, and most of all, fulfilling career. We want you to take control of your own career path now so that in a few years you'll be able to say you are where you want to be—not just in some job where you ended up.

Remember, always be your authentic self. Don't be swayed by what other people think you should be, or do. Ultimately, if you aren't happy, you will be incapable of bringing happiness to others. Trust that your interests will lead you to the career of your dreams. Success doesn't happen spontaneously. It is the combination of life lessons and experiences that, when put together, create the building blocks of a successful career.

We intended to create a handbook for young professionals that would share the secrets to success and insights that hold true across most industries. But we also wanted it to be specifically about you. So we asked almost as many questions as we answered. Reading this book also takes some work because you have to answer some tough questions as you go through it.

After reading *Grad to Great*, you may put it away for a bit, and we hope you will continue to reference it. We wrote this book with the expectation that some tips would be useful to you now, and some in one or five years' time. We sincerely hope you find it more useful every time you read it.

Best of luck to you, and please visit us on our web site www.gradtogreat.com to let us know how you're doing.

Sample Cover Letter

October 4, 2008

Mrs. Jane Employer
President
XYZ Publishing Company
1234 Main Street
Rochester Hills, MI 48309

Dear Mrs. Employer,

We met when you came to speak to my journalism class at Northwestern University last Tuesday. I very much enjoyed your speech and I am now even more excited about pursuing a career in publishing. As I mentioned, I am very interested in the entry-level position in Sales and Marketing that you have available. I have attached my resumé per your request.

I will be graduating in December 2008 with a Bachelor of Arts degree in Business Administration. I am extremely hard working and am very aware that I know little to nothing about publishing. I am, however, a very fast learner, and have always wanted to work in the publishing industry. I have a great attitude and am willing to work as many hours as you need me. I am also proficient at working with Apple Macintosh computers, which I understand is what you use at your offices.

In addition to my resumé, I have included a list of my references for your convenience. I would very much appreciate the opportunity to discuss this position with you in person. Please feel free to call me at 555-555-5551 at any time.

Thank you very much for your consideration.

Best regards,

Samantha Smith
5555 State Street
Chicago, IL 60601
555-555-5555
Samantha@gradtogreat,com

Sample Letter

October 4, 2008

Mr. John Employer
President
XYZ Interactive Media Company
1234 Oak Street
Oak Park, IL 60302

Dear Mr. Employer,

My name is Jane Smith I am writing because I have been a fan of your firm throughout my college career. I admire the web sites you built for DEF Company, and GHII. They are both truly amazing. I am writing to you because I would love the opportunity to work for you as an entry-level graphic designer. I am also open to starting out as an intern and working my way up, or any other type of arrangement that you deem appropriate.

During my internship with ABC Media Company, I gained experience with the following programs: Flash, Illustrator, Photoshop, HTML, Fireworks, and Dreamweaver. I have a Bachelor of Arts degree in Graphic Design from Georgia Tech. I have great references, and would really appreciate the opportunity to discuss this with you further. Please feel free to call me at either of the numbers below if you would like to discuss this proposal. I tried to make this as short as possible because I know you are probably very busy.

Thank you for your consideration. I have attached my resumé and references for your review, and would be delighted to show you my portfolio.

Best regards,

Jane Smith
5555 Main Street
Atlanta, GA 30332
555-555-5555
Jane@gradtogreat.com

ABOUT THE AUTHORS

Anne Brown is a communications professional with 11 years of experience in journalism, marketing, higher education, and project management. Anne earned her B.A. in English from Michigan State University, and received her MBA from Loyola University in Chicago. She is an alumnus of the Executive Scholar program at the Kellogg School of Management at Northwestern University.

Anne lives with her husband, Aaron, in Chicago, IL. She is an active member of the National Association of Women Business Owners.

Beth Zefo works for General Motors, leading the Labor Relations and Hourly Employment team, in Atlanta, GA. During the past 10 years, she has held various positions in several functional areas throughout the auto industry including: supply chain management, supplier quality engineering, new product launch, corporate communications, and personnel. Beth graduated from Michigan State University with a B.S. from the College of Engineering. She received her MBA from the Owen Graduate School of Management at Vanderbilt University.

Beth lives with her husband, Derek, in Mableton, GA. She is an active member of the Junior League of Atlanta.

Together Anne and Beth run Brockseker Communications LLC, a consulting firm offering presentations and workshops for companies and universities on a variety of professional development topics including half and full-day Grad to Great™ seminars.

This title may be purchased in bulk for business or promotional use. For special sales information, please write:

Special Markets Department - Dalidaze Press
1400 W. Devon Avenue
Suite 407
Chicago, IL 60660

specialmarkets@dalidazepress.com